The Quantum Code of the Spirit
A Journey Between Particles and Perception

Kai Lian

Título Original:
The Quantum Code of the Spirit
Copyright © 2025, publicado por Luiz Antonio dos Santos ME.
Este livro é uma obra de não-ficção que explora práticas e conceitos no campo da espiritualidade quântica e da consciência. Através de uma abordagem transdisciplinar, o autor oferece uma síntese entre física moderna e sabedorias ancestrais, com ferramentas para expansão da percepção, equilíbrio energético e transformação interior.

1ª Edição
Equipe de Produção
Autor: Kai Lian
Editor: Luiz Santos
Capa: Studios Booklas / Aline Trevas
Consultor: Nivaldo Térion
Pesquisadores: Selma Dranor / Érico Venn / Tadeu Ramm
Diagramação: Lorena Quarx

Publicação e Identificação
The Quantum Code of the Spirit
Booklas, 2025
Categorias: Espiritualidade Quântica / Ciência e Consciência
DDC: 299.93 — Espiritualidade comparada e novas religiões
CDU: 133.9 — Fenômenos psíquicos e ocultismo em geral

Todos os direitos reservados a:
Luiz Antonio dos Santos ME / Booklas
Nenhuma parte deste livro pode ser reproduzida, armazenada num sistema de recuperação ou transmitida por qualquer meio — eletrônico, mecânico, fotocópia, gravação ou outro — sem a autorização prévia e expressa do detentor dos direitos de autorais.

Summary

Systematic Index 5
Prologue 10
Chapter 1 Universal Energy 14
Chapter 2 The Nature of Consciousness 22
Chapter 3 The Nature of Reality 29
Chapter 4 Matter and Spirit 36
Chapter 5 The Quantum Revolution 43
Chapter 6 Wave-Particle Duality 49
Chapter 7 Quantum Uncertainty 55
Chapter 8 The Observer 61
Chapter 9 Collapse of the Wave Function 67
Chapter 10 Non-Locality 73
Chapter 11 Quantum Entanglement 79
Chapter 12 Cosmic Unity 84
Chapter 13 The Unified Field 90
Chapter 14 Morphogenetic Fields 95
Chapter 15 Collective Consciousness 101
Chapter 16 Non-Local Mind 107
Chapter 17 Beyond Space-Time 113
Chapter 18 Multidimensionality 118
Chapter 19 Holographic Universe 124
Chapter 20 Quantum Consciousness 130
Chapter 21 Consciousness Beyond the Body 136

Chapter 22	The Power of Intention	143
Chapter 23	Manifestation	149
Chapter 24	Quantum Healing	155
Chapter 25	Expansion of Consciousness	161
Chapter 26	Synchronicity	168
Chapter 27	Ancient Wisdom	173
Chapter 28	Current Convergence	179
Chapter 29	Practical Applications	185
Chapter 30	Evolution of Consciousness	190
Chapter 31	Cosmic Purpose	196
Chapter 32	Quantum Awakening	202
Chapter 33	Quantum Soul	207
Epilogue		212

Systematic Index

Chapter 1: Universal Energy - Establishes the fundamental principle that everything in the universe is energy, linking modern science and ancient wisdom.

Chapter 2: The Nature of Consciousness - Explores the mystery of consciousness, contrasting scientific views on the brain with spiritual perspectives on the soul or spirit.

Chapter 3: The Nature of Reality - Questions the objective nature of reality, discussing perceptual limits, quantum physics implications, and the concept of Maya.

Chapter 4: Matter and Spirit - Discusses the traditional divide between matter and spirit, proposing their unity as different vibrational states of energy.

Chapter 5: The Quantum Revolution - Describes the historical shift from classical physics to quantum mechanics, introducing key discoveries and groundbreaking concepts.

Chapter 6: Wave-Particle Duality - Explains the paradoxical quantum concept where entities exhibit both wave and particle behaviors, illustrated by the double-slit experiment.

Chapter 7: Quantum Uncertainty - Introduces Heisenberg's Uncertainty Principle, exploring its implications for determinism, probability, and the inherent fuzziness of reality.

Chapter 8: The Observer - Discusses the crucial and active role of the observer in quantum mechanics, suggesting consciousness participates in shaping reality.

Chapter 9: Collapse of the Wave Function - Examines the process by which quantum possibilities become definite reality upon measurement, touching upon Schrödinger's Cat paradox.

Chapter 10: Non-Locality - Explains the concept of instantaneous connection at a distance, confirmed by experiments violating Bell's inequalities, challenging locality.

Chapter 11: Quantum Entanglement - Details the phenomenon where particles become intrinsically linked, acting as a single system regardless of spatial separation.

Chapter 12: Cosmic Unity - Argues for the fundamental interconnectedness of the universe, drawing from quantum non-locality, cosmology, and spiritual holistic views.

Chapter 13: The Unified Field - Explores the scientific quest for a Theory of Everything and the spiritual concept of a primordial field underlying all existence.

Chapter 14: Morphogenetic Fields - Presents Rupert Sheldrake's theory of morphic fields and resonance guiding form and behavior through a collective memory in nature.

Chapter 15: Collective Consciousness - Discusses concepts like Jung's Collective Unconscious and

Teilhard's Noosphere, suggesting a shared mental field connecting humanity.

Chapter 16: Non-Local Mind - Investigates evidence for psi phenomena like telepathy and remote viewing, suggesting the mind may operate beyond the brain's physical limits.

Chapter 17: Beyond Space-Time - Explores evidence and concepts suggesting consciousness might transcend linear time, including precognition and physics' hints about time's nature.

Chapter 18: Multidimensionality - Considers the possibility of extra spatial dimensions or parallel universes proposed by physics and echoed in spiritual cosmologies.

Chapter 19: Holographic Universe - Introduces the hypothesis that reality operates holographically, where each part contains information about the whole, linking physics and neuroscience.

Chapter 20: Quantum Consciousness - Examines theories attempting to explain consciousness through quantum mechanics, such as Orch OR, panpsychism, and quantum idealism.

Chapter 21: Consciousness Beyond the Body - Addresses the possibility of consciousness surviving physical death, analyzing Near-Death Experiences and past-life memory research.

Chapter 22: The Power of Intention - Explores whether focused thought and intention can influence physical reality, discussing psychokinesis research and the placebo effect.

Chapter 23: Manifestation - Discusses the concept of consciously creating desired reality through inner alignment and principles like the Law of Attraction.

Chapter 24: Quantum Healing - Presents a holistic view of health, integrating the mind-body connection, placebo effect, spontaneous remission, and energy healing modalities.

Chapter 25: Expansion of Consciousness - Describes methods like meditation, yoga, and breathwork for achieving expanded states of awareness and mystical experiences.

Chapter 26: Synchronicity - Explains Carl Jung's concept of meaningful coincidences, suggesting an acausal connecting principle operating through meaning.

Chapter 27: Ancient Wisdom - Highlights parallels between modern quantum insights and perennial truths found in Vedanta, Buddhism, Taoism, and other spiritual traditions.

Chapter 28: Current Convergence - Discusses the contemporary movement towards integrating science and spirituality, citing key institutions, researchers, and cultural trends as of 2025.

Chapter 29: Practical Applications - Offers ways to apply the book's insights in daily life, focusing on intention, energy management, empathy, and holistic health.

Chapter 30: Evolution of Consciousness - Proposes that consciousness evolves individually and collectively, potentially moving towards an integrated, holistic stage.

Chapter 31: Cosmic Purpose - Explores the question of purpose behind existence, considering fine-tuning in physics alongside spiritual views on self-experience and growth.

Chapter 32: Quantum Awakening - Suggests humanity is potentially undergoing a collective shift in consciousness, catalyzed by the convergence of science and spirituality.

Chapter 33: Quantum Soul - Synthesizes the view of the human being as an energetic, conscious, interconnected, participatory, and evolving entity integrated with the cosmos.

Prologue

You are about to embark on a journey that doesn't just inform—it transforms.

What you hold in your hands is no ordinary book. It is a portal. A link between the visible and the invisible, between what you think you are and what you truly are. Here, you will not find mere bound pages, but layers of meaning, pulsations of wisdom that traverse centuries, reverberate in the quantum fields of modern science, and echo in the silence of the awakened soul.

Allow yourself to cross this frontier.

We live in times when reality seems hardened, when Cartesian logic attempts to imprison the infinite in fixed formulas. But there is a silent call—profound, intimate—emanating from that which pulses beyond matter, beyond the rational mind. A call that awakens only in attentive hearts, curious minds, and spirits thirsty for truth. This call doesn't come from outside. It is born within you. And that is precisely why this book found its way into your hands.

Everything is energy. Everything vibrates. Everything is connected.

These are not poetic affirmations, but findings anchored both in the principles of quantum physics and in the ancestral teachings of great spiritual traditions.

Here, the author does not speculate—he reveals. He does not propose a belief, but invites direct experience. The experience of perceiving yourself not as a fragmented being, but as an active part of a field of consciousness that interpenetrates all reality.

You feel there is something more. You always have.

The silent restlessness in the face of everyday superficiality, the intuition that events are not random, the impression that your mind influences matter—none of this is illusion. It is the prelude to an awakening. The reading that begins now is a powerful confirmation that your intuition was right all along.

As you turn these pages, you will discover you are not separate from the universe—you are the universe experiencing itself in human form. The energy that moves galaxies is the same that vibrates in your thoughts, emotions, breath. The consciousness that observes is the same that creates. There are no barriers between the micro and the macro. There are no boundaries between science and spirituality. There is unity. There is coherence. There is meaning.

This book connects points that, for a long time, were kept distant:

– Quantum physics and meditation.
– Energy fields and states of consciousness.
– Wave-particle duality and the human soul.
– The scientific observer and the inner observer.

This fusion is not forced. It is natural. It is inevitable. And, upon recognizing it, you will perceive that reality is much more malleable, alive, and interactive than you were ever taught.

Yes, your mind influences the world.

Yes, your emotions create vibrations that shape events.

Yes, you are a co-creator of reality.

This is not an invitation to escape the real world, but to dive deeper into it. To true participation. To conscious presence. The work you are about to explore is a rare synthesis of scientific clarity and spiritual depth. There are no dogmas here. There are revelations. There are no empty promises. There are maps, instruments, directions. Each chapter is a step—or rather, a frequency—that resonates with your own evolution.

You will feel it.

You will not just understand with the intellect, but with your entire being. Like when music touches something no explanation can reach. Like when a gaze awakens memories not of this life. The reading will be less a process and more a recognition. A remembering of who you are, what you have always been, and what you can still become.

You will be challenged, yes. Because what is being offered here is freedom. And freedom requires courage. The courage to question. To observe yourself. To reconstruct yourself. The courage to abandon certainties to access a greater truth.

This book is for those who sense that reality is more than it appears.

For those who feel that science need not deny the spirit.

For those who know, deep down, that the soul pulses at a quantum frequency.

For you.

Upon entering this vibrational space of knowledge, you will not just be reading—you will be read. Each paragraph will echo in levels of your being you might not even know how to name. And, by the end, you will not be the same.

Accept this invitation not with the eyes of reason, but with the wholeness of your being.

And remember: the universe always responds to intention.

The question is not "Is this real?".

The question is: Are you ready to remember?

Luiz Santos

Editor

Chapter 1
Universal Energy

Imagine, for a moment, the universe in its unimaginable vastness. Galaxies swirl in cosmic dances lasting billions of years, stars are born and die in explosions of light and power, planets orbit distant suns, some perhaps harboring life forms we cannot even conceive. Now, think of our own world: pulsating oceans, vibrant forests, imposing mountains sculpted by time. Look at your own hands, feel the pulse in your chest, the breath moving in and out. All of this, from the largest galaxy to the smallest cell in your body, shares a fundamental truth, a common essence that permeates every fiber of existence.

Everything is energy. This statement might sound simple, almost trivial, but its implications are profound, revolutionary. It holds the key to unlocking not only the mysteries of the cosmos but also the mysteries of our own consciousness, our soul.

Our everyday experience presents us with a world of solid objects, separate from one another. We feel the solidity of the chair we sit on, the rigidity of the table where we rest our arms, the consistency of the floor beneath our feet. We perceive ourselves as distinct physical entities, bounded by our skin. This perception, while useful for our survival and daily interaction, is, on a more fundamental level, a sensory illusion.

Modern science, especially twentieth-century physics, has revealed a radically different picture of matter. When we investigate what makes up this apparent solidity, we find atoms. For a long time, we imagined atoms as tiny, solid spheres, like microscopic billiard balls. However, later discoveries revealed a surprising picture. An atom is, in fact, almost entirely empty space. At the center lies a minuscule nucleus, containing protons and neutrons, and far from it, electrons orbit at incredibly high speeds. If we enlarged an atom to the size of a football stadium, the nucleus would be smaller than a grain of sand at the center of the field, and the electrons would be even smaller particles spinning in the highest stands. The rest? Emptiness. An emptiness that corresponds to more than 99.99% of the atom's total volume.

So, what fills this vast "void"? What gives the illusion of solidity to the world? The answer lies in energy fields. The space within and around atoms is not truly empty; it pulses with electromagnetic force fields and other quantum fields. It is these fields, interacting with each other, that create the sensation of resistance, of touch, of substance. Electrons, for example, are not just particles but also manifestations of energy fields extending through space. Their rapid movement and the forces they exert create a kind of energy barrier that prevents one atom from easily passing through another. When you touch an object, your electrons are repelling the electrons of the object. You are not touching solid "matter" in the classical sense, but rather interacting with force fields, with vibrational patterns of energy. The solidity we perceive is the macroscopic result of these energetic interactions on a microscopic scale.

Therefore, the chair, the table, your own body, everything that seems dense and concrete, is actually a complex arrangement of energy vibrating at different frequencies, condensed into stable patterns that our senses interpret as matter.

This understanding was thrust into the scientific spotlight by Albert Einstein in the early twentieth century with his famous equation $E=mc^2$. Although often associated with nuclear energy, its meaning is much more universal and philosophical. The equation establishes a fundamental equivalence between energy (E) and mass (m), connected by the speed of light squared (c^2), a cosmic constant of immense value. This means that mass is not something separate from energy; mass *is* a form of energy, highly concentrated energy, frozen into the form of matter. Conversely, energy can convert into mass. They are two faces of the same universal coin. All matter in the universe, from stardust to your body, is a colossal reservoir of primordial energy. A small gram of matter contains an amount of energy equivalent to that released by a large nuclear explosion.

This interchangeability is not just theoretical; it occurs constantly in nature, such as inside stars, where mass is converted into light and heat, and in particle accelerators, where pure energy can give rise to particles of matter. Einstein's vision dissolved the ancient dichotomy between the "material" and the "energetic," revealing a universe where everything is, at its root, dynamic energy.

What is fascinating is that this revolutionary view from modern science finds deep echoes in spiritual and philosophical traditions that flourished millennia before Einstein and quantum physics. Ancient cultures, through introspection, meditation, and subtle observation of nature, seem to have intuited this fundamental truth.

In Hinduism, we find the concept of *Prana*. Prana is not simply breath but the universal life force, the subtle energy that animates all living beings and fills the entire cosmos. It is the energy that flows through subtle channels in the body (*nadis*) and concentrates in energy centers (*chakras*), being essential for physical, mental, and spiritual health. Practices like Yoga and *Pranayama* (breath control) are designed to harmonize and increase the flow of Prana in the individual, connecting them to the cosmic source of this energy.

In traditional Chinese medicine and Taoism, we find a similar concept called *Chi* (or Qi). Chi is the vital energy that flows through everything in the universe. In the human body, it circulates through meridians, and its balanced flow is considered essential for health. Practices like Acupuncture, Tai Chi Chuan, and Qigong aim precisely to unblock and harmonize the flow of Chi, promoting well-being and longevity. For Taoists, the universe itself was born from the *Wu Ji* (the primordial void, pure potential), differentiating into Yin and Yang, two energetic polarities whose dynamic interaction generates the "ten thousand things," that is, all manifestation. Chi is the expression of this fundamental energetic dynamic.

Other traditions speak of analogous concepts: the Egyptians spoke of *Ka*, the Greeks of *Pneuma*, the Hawaiian kahunas of *Mana*. Many indigenous traditions of the Americas speak of the Great Spirit or a vital force that permeates mountains, rivers, plants, and animals. In various Western mystical currents, we find the idea of Divine Light, Ether, or Universal Spirit as the primordial substance of creation.

What all these visions share is the perception of an invisible yet real and fundamental energy that sustains and animates the physical world. They describe a reality where dense matter emerges from a subtler energetic substrate, a life force that connects all things. God, or the Primordial Source, in many of these views, is not just a distant creator but the omnipresent energy itself that constitutes the essence of everything that exists. "God is Light," "God is Love," are expressions that, beyond their moral sense, may also point to this energetic and vibrational nature of divinity as the foundation of reality.

Now, we can begin to build a bridge between these two great avenues of human knowledge: modern science and ancient wisdom. Physics tells us that matter is 99.99% empty space filled with vibrating energy fields and that mass is condensed energy ($E=mc^2$). Spiritual traditions tell us that the physical world is a manifestation of a universal vital energy (Prana, Chi, Divine Light) and that apparent reality can be an illusion (*Maya*, in Hinduism) that conceals an underlying energetic unity. Do they not seem to be speaking of aspects of the same fundamental truth, using different languages shaped by their times and methodologies?

Science describes this energy in terms of fields, particles, frequencies, and vibrations. Spirituality describes it in terms of life force, consciousness, light, and spirit. Perhaps matter and spirit are not opposing entities, but rather different vibrational states of the same universal energy. Matter would be energy vibrating at lower, denser frequencies, becoming perceptible to our physical senses. Spirit, consciousness, life force, would be this same energy vibrating at higher, subtler frequencies, generally imperceptible to our common instruments and senses, but accessible through intuition, meditation, inner experience.

Imagine a spectrum of vibrations. At one end, we have energy so dense that it manifests as rock, metal, flesh, and bone. As the vibrational frequency increases, this energy becomes subtler: water, air, sound, visible light, radio waves, X-rays, gamma rays. And beyond that? Could the spectrum continue to even higher frequencies, corresponding to the realms of thought, emotion, consciousness, spirit? Quantum physics, with its discoveries about wave-particle duality and fundamental interconnectedness, opens doors for us to seriously consider this possibility. It forces us to abandon the mechanistic view of a universe made of solid, separate parts, and invites us to embrace a vision of a universe as a vast ocean of vibrant energy, a unified field where everything is interconnected and in constant flux.

Understanding that everything is energy is the first fundamental step in our journey to explore the "Quantum Soul." This understanding dissolves the apparent barrier between the physical and non-physical, between science and spirituality, between mind and matter. It provides us with a new lexicon, a new way of thinking about ourselves and the universe. When we talk about "raising our vibration," "tuning into good energies," or "feeling the energy of a place or person," perhaps we are not just using poetic metaphors. Perhaps we are touching upon a literal description of the underlying reality.

If everything is energy, and if energy possesses frequency and vibration, then our thoughts, emotions, and state of consciousness are also energetic vibrational patterns. And if quantum physics shows us that energy can be influenced by observation and intention, this opens an extraordinary range of possibilities about how our own consciousness can interact with the energetic universe around us and within us.

This chapter lays the foundation stone. Accepting the premise that the universe is fundamentally energetic allows us to begin exploring the deeper questions: What is consciousness in this energetic context? How does it arise? How does it interact with matter? What is the true nature of the reality we perceive?

By uniting the precision of scientific language (energy, frequency, vibration, fields) with the depth of spiritual wisdom (Prana, Chi, life force, Divine Light), we prepare the ground for a fascinating investigation into the intrinsic connection between our soul and the quantum fabric of the cosmos. We are about to embark on an exploration that can transform not only our understanding of the world but also our experience of life, revealing our innate potential as energetic co-creators of our reality. The journey begins now, anchored in this simple and powerful truth: everything is energy.

Chapter 2
The Nature of Consciousness

If everything in the universe, from cosmic dust to biological complexity, is fundamentally energy in different forms and vibrations, then the most intimate and perhaps most perplexing question of all arises: what is this "thing" that perceives, that feels, that experiences all this energy? What are *we* in this vast energetic ocean? In short, what is consciousness?

This question has echoed through the halls of philosophy, science, and spirituality for millennia, resisting easy answers, remaining one of the greatest enigmas of existence. It is the inner light that illuminates our experience of the world, the sense of "being," the fact that we are not just automatons processing information, but subjects experiencing a reality. Without consciousness, the universe might exist as a complex and empty mechanism, but it would be devoid of meaning, beauty, pain, or joy. It is consciousness that gives color, sound, texture, and meaning to the tapestry of existence.

When we try to define consciousness, we often struggle to describe what is most fundamental to our experience. Consciousness is the capacity to experience, to be aware. It is the subjective quality of "what it is like to be" something or someone. It is the difference between a thermostat reacting to temperature and you *feeling* cold. It is the difference between a camera registering the color red and you *seeing* red, with all its vividness and possible emotional associations. This intrinsic quality of experience, this phenomenal aspect, is often called *qualia* by philosophers. How do you describe the sweetness of honey to someone who has never tasted it? How do you explain the melancholy of a song or the euphoria of an achievement? These are direct experiences, felt from the inside out, constituting the core of what it means to be conscious.

This intrinsic subjectivity makes consciousness a unique challenge for science, which traditionally deals with the objective, the measurable, the observable from the outside. Modern science, particularly neuroscience, has made remarkable progress in mapping the correlations between brain activity and conscious states. We know that certain brain areas are associated with vision, others with hearing, others with planning, emotions, language. Damage to specific regions can drastically alter personality, memory, or the very capacity to be conscious. Technologies like functional magnetic resonance imaging (fMRI) allow us to observe which parts of the brain "light up" when we think, feel, or perceive something. This intimate connection between the physical brain and subjective experience is undeniable.

For many scientists, this strongly suggests that consciousness is a product of brain activity, an emergent property of the complex network of billions of neurons firing in intricate patterns. In this materialistic view, the brain *creates* consciousness, much like the kidneys produce urine or the stomach produces acid. The mind, then, would be what the brain does.

However, this explanation, though dominant in many scientific circles, leaves a crucial gap, a deep mystery that philosopher David Chalmers famously dubbed "the hard problem of consciousness." The "easy problems" (which are actually immensely complex) involve explaining the functions of consciousness: how the brain processes information, directs attention, controls behavior, stores memories. The "hard problem" is explaining *why* and *how* all this physical neuronal activity gives rise to subjective experience, to qualia. Why should all this biological computation *feel* like anything? Why couldn't we be "philosophical zombies" – beings that process information and behave exactly like us, but with no inner experience, no light turned on inside? Neuroscience can show *which* neurons fire when we see red, but it doesn't explain *why* this specific firing is accompanied by the subjective *sensation* of red. This leap from physical matter to subjective experience remains an explanatory abyss, the great mystery at the heart of the science of mind.

This difficulty in reducing consciousness solely to brain activity has led some scientists and philosophers to question whether the brain is truly the exclusive generator of consciousness. Could the relationship be more subtle? An analogy often used is that of a television or radio set. The device picks up signals transmitted through the air and converts them into image and sound. The music is not *inside* the radio; it merely tunes into and expresses it. Similarly, could we think of the brain not as the creator of consciousness, but as a complex receiver and transmitter, a biological tuner that picks up and modulates a broader consciousness, perhaps a field of consciousness that permeates the universe, akin to the energy field discussed in the previous chapter?

In this perspective, the brain would be the necessary hardware for consciousness to manifest and interact in the three-dimensional physical world, but consciousness itself could have a more fundamental origin, not exclusively locatable within the skull. This view offers a conceptual framework that could potentially accommodate phenomena challenging the purely cerebral view, such as lucid near-death experiences occurring during cardiac arrest, or certain psychic experiences suggesting a mind not confined to the body (topics we will explore later). It's not about denying the crucial importance of the brain, but reconsidering its exact function in the consciousness equation.

Here, again, we find a remarkable resonance with millennial spiritual perspectives. For countless traditions around the globe, consciousness is not a late epiphenomenon of material evolution, but the primordial element, the very essence of existence. What science calls "consciousness," spirituality often calls *Soul* (*Atman* in Hinduism, *Psyche* in ancient Greece, *Nephesh* in Judaism) or *Spirit*. This Soul is seen as the divine spark within each being, the immortal and unchanging part of us that observes the flow of life, learns from experiences, and persists beyond the death of the physical body. The body and brain are considered temporary vehicles for the expression and evolution of this essential consciousness in the material plane.

Consciousness, in this view, does not emerge from matter; on the contrary, matter can be seen as a manifestation or expression of fundamental consciousness. The universe would not be a machine that accidentally produced consciousness, but rather a field of consciousness manifesting as a universe. God, or the Ultimate Source, is often conceived as Pure Consciousness, and we, as individuals, would be individualized expressions of this Cosmic Consciousness.

This perspective invites us to look within, to seek the "I" that experiences behind the fleeting thoughts, emotions, and sensations. Who is it that observes your thoughts arising and disappearing? Who perceives your joys and sorrows? Meditative practices in various traditions aim precisely to cultivate this self-observation, to differentiate the silent observer (the inner Self, the witness) from the content of the mind (the constant stream of thoughts and perceptions). This inner observer is often associated with the *Higher Self* or the *Divine Spark*, our direct connection to universal consciousness. It is the part of us that remains serene and lucid even amidst the turmoil of life, the source of our innate intuition, wisdom, and compassion. Recognizing and connecting with this core of pure consciousness is seen as the path to self-understanding, inner peace, and spiritual enlightenment.

Therefore, the nature of consciousness presents itself as a crucial point of convergence and dialogue between science and spirituality. Science, with its methodological rigor, maps the physical correlates of consciousness and confronts the "hard problem," acknowledging the current limits of its understanding of subjective experience. Spirituality, through millennia of introspective exploration, offers a vision of consciousness as fundamental, as the essence of being and the source of reality, proposing paths for its direct exploration and expansion.

Neither approach, in isolation, seems to hold the complete answer. Perhaps the truth lies in integration, in recognizing that consciousness has both a physical aspect, anchored in brain function, and a subtler, transcendent aspect, possibly connected to a universal field of energy and information.

Understanding consciousness is, ultimately, understanding ourselves at our deepest level. It is the key to unlocking our relationship with the energetic universe we inhabit. If our consciousness is not strictly limited to the brain, if it can interact with energy fields, if it is an individualized expression of a greater Consciousness, then the implications are immense. This opens the door to understanding how our thoughts and intentions might influence reality, how we can connect with each other and the cosmos in subtle ways, and what our greater purpose might be in this existential journey.

The investigation into the nature of consciousness is not just an academic or philosophical exercise; it is a vital exploration that touches the core of our being and defines our perception of who we are and what is possible. By keeping an open mind to the discoveries of science and the wisdom of spiritual traditions, we can begin to glimpse a more complete and integrated picture of this mysterious light that animates us, the flame of consciousness burning at the heart of the universe and within each of us. The journey to understand the Quantum Soul inevitably passes through unraveling the secrets of this conscious essence.

Chapter 3
The Nature of Reality

Having explored the fundamental idea that everything is energy and questioned the nature of the consciousness that perceives this energy, we are naturally led to inquire about the very nature of what we call "reality." What is real? Does the world we experience – with its landscapes, objects, other people – exist exactly as we perceive it, independent of us? Or does our perception, our consciousness, play an active role in constructing what we take for reality? This question, as old as philosophy itself, gains new nuances and urgency in light of modern physics discoveries and the profound intuitions of spiritual traditions. Challenging our assumptions about reality is a crucial step in understanding our place and power within the cosmos.

The prevailing view, both in common sense and in the classical science that has shaped our civilization for centuries, is that of an objective reality. In this perspective, the universe exists "out there," solid, factual, governed by immutable laws, completely independent of who observes it. A stone is a stone, with its properties of mass, texture, and chemical composition, whether someone is looking at it or not.

Time flows uniformly, space is a fixed stage where events unfold. Reality is seen as something concrete and external, and our task, as observers or scientists, is to discover its laws and describe it as accurately as possible. Our senses, though imperfect, are windows onto this pre-existing external world.

This mechanistic and materialistic view, consolidated by thinkers like Isaac Newton, was incredibly successful in explaining and predicting phenomena in the macroscopic world, leading to technological advances that transformed our society. It offers us a sense of order, predictability, and control over the natural world.

However, even within this classical view, we must acknowledge the inherent limitations of our perception. Our senses are highly specialized biological tools, evolved to ensure our survival in a specific environment, not to capture the totality of reality. We perceive only a tiny sliver of the electromagnetic spectrum as visible light, ignoring radio waves, microwaves, infrared, ultraviolet, X-rays, and gamma rays that permeate the space around us. Our ears pick up a limited range of sound frequencies; we don't hear the ultrasounds of bats or the infrasounds of elephants. Our sense of smell and taste are rudimentary compared to those of many other animals.

What we perceive as a continuous and stable world is actually a reconstruction made by our brain from fragmented and limited sensory signals. The brain interprets, filters, fills in gaps, and projects expectations based on past experiences and cultural conditioning.

Optical illusions vividly demonstrate how our perception can be deceived, how the brain actively constructs visual reality. A colorblind person perceives the world differently. A dog, with its highly acute sense of smell, lives in an olfactory universe we can barely imagine. Therefore, even without leaving the traditional scientific paradigm, we already have indications that our perceived "reality" is an edited version, a subjective model based on incomplete sensory data and neural processing. We do not experience the world directly as it "is," but rather an interpretation of it.

This notion of a not-so-fixed and objective reality was drastically amplified by the discoveries of quantum physics in the early twentieth century. By investigating the subatomic realm, scientists encountered phenomena that completely defied classical intuition. Particles like electrons seemed not to have definite properties, such as position or momentum, until they were measured. Before measurement, they existed only as waves of probability, a field of potentialities. The very act of observing seemed to influence the outcome, "collapsing" the probability wave into a definite state. This suggested that, at the most fundamental level, reality is not fixed and predetermined, but probabilistic and, somehow, dependent on the observer. The image of an objective and independent universe "out there" began to dissolve, giving way to a stranger, more interconnected view, where observer and observed seem intrinsically linked. Although quantum effects are generally subtle on our macroscopic scale, they reveal a fundamental nature of reality that differs radically from

Newton's solid and predictable world. Quantum physics opened a crack in the concept of objective reality, suggesting it might be more malleable, more participatory than we imagined.

This idea that perceived reality may not be the ultimate reality, or that our mind participates in its creation, finds striking parallels in ancient spiritual traditions, especially Eastern philosophies. In Hinduism and Buddhism, the concept of *Maya* describes the veil of illusion that conceals the true nature of reality. Maya is the cosmic power that makes the phenomenal world – the world of names and forms, of separate objects and transient events – seem real and substantial. Under the veil of Maya, we perceive multiplicity and separation, forgetting the underlying unity (*Brahman*, in Hinduism) or the empty and interdependent nature of all phenomena (*Shunyata*, in Buddhism).

Maya doesn't necessarily mean the world is a complete hallucination or doesn't exist at all. Rather, it means our habitual perception of it is misleading, that we mistake appearances for essence, the transient for the permanent, the fragmented for the whole. The apparent solidity of objects, the fixedness of our self, the linearity of time – all this would be part of the illusion woven by Maya, a mental construct that traps us in a cycle of suffering (*samsara*) until we awaken to the true nature of reality through wisdom and spiritual practice.

Modern physics' discovery that solid objects are actually vast empty spaces filled with probabilistic energy fields seems to echo, in a surprising way, this ancient spiritual notion that the solidity of the material world is a perceptual illusion.

Bringing together these perspectives – the limitations of sensory perception, the implications of quantum physics, and the wisdom of traditions like the one speaking of Maya – a picture of reality emerges as a complex construction. What we experience as the "real world" appears to be the result of an intricate interaction between an underlying energetic potential (described by quantum physics), the filters of our biological senses, the interpretive processing of our brain (shaped by evolution, culture, and personal experience), and, crucially, the state of our own consciousness.

We are not mere passive spectators of a cosmic movie unfolding independently of us. We are, somehow, active participants in the very weaving of the tapestry of reality we experience. Our beliefs, expectations, focuses of attention, and emotional states can act as additional filters, coloring our perception and perhaps even subtly influencing the events that manifest in our lives.

Some spiritual and philosophical currents go even further, proposing that physical reality is not just interpreted or influenced by consciousness, but projected by it. In this idealist view, consciousness would be the primary reality, and the material world a secondary manifestation, like a dream or a mental projection of a greater Cosmic Mind, or even of our own collective consciousness. The universe would, in this sense, be a reflection of the consciousness that perceives it. Although this idea might seem radical from a materialistic standpoint, it finds support in mystical experiences where individuals report feeling unity with everything and perceiving the world as an emanation of their own expanded consciousness. Quantum physics, by demonstrating the role of the observer, while not directly proving idealism, certainly makes this perspective less implausible than it was in the classical paradigm.

Perhaps a more balanced and integrative view is that of interdependence. Reality would be neither purely objective (existing independently of consciousness) nor purely subjective (being just a projection of the mind), but rather emerging from the dynamic *relationship* between consciousness and the field of quantum potentiality. The universe offers a range of energetic possibilities, and consciousness, through the act of observing, perceiving, and intending, participates in actualizing these possibilities into concrete experience. Observer and observed co-create reality moment by moment, in a cosmic dance of energy and consciousness. This view resonates both with certain interpretations of quantum mechanics (like the relational interpretation) and with holistic philosophies emphasizing interconnection and participation.

Regardless of which interpretation seems most convincing to us, the central point is the invitation to question our certainties about the nature of reality. The world may be far more mysterious, fluid, and participatory than our everyday view leads us to believe. Solidity might be an energetic illusion, separation a perceptual veil, and our own consciousness might play a much more central role in the orchestration of existence than we ever imagined.

Recognizing this does not lead to nihilism or denial of the world, but rather to a posture of greater humility, wonder, and responsibility. If we participate in constructing our reality, then the quality of our consciousness, of our thoughts and intentions, becomes fundamental. Opening our minds to the possibility of a malleable, interconnected reality permeated by consciousness is essential for understanding the phenomena we will explore in the upcoming chapters, such as the power of the observer, non-locality, and the mind's ability to influence matter. The journey to the Quantum Soul requires us to dare to look beyond the veil of apparent reality and contemplate the profound dance between the inner universe and the outer universe.

Chapter 4
Matter and Spirit

Throughout the history of human thought, a deep divide has often separated our understanding of the world into two seemingly distinct domains: that of matter and that of spirit. On one side, we have the realm of the physical, the tangible, the measurable – the traditional domain of science. It's the world of stones, trees, bodies, stars, everything we can touch, weigh, analyze in its chemical and physical components. On the other side, we have the realm of the immaterial, the intangible, the sacred – the traditional domain of religion, philosophy, and inner experience. It's the world of consciousness, soul, feelings, ideas, faith, God.

This dichotomy, this sense that matter and spirit are fundamentally different substances, perhaps even opposites, has profoundly shaped our culture, our institutions, and our very perception of who we are. But is this separation real? Or could it be another perceptual illusion, a mental construct preventing us from seeing a deeper, unified connection in the tapestry of existence?

This division was particularly crystallized in Western thought by the French philosopher René Descartes in the 17th century. Descartes proposed a radical dualism between *res extensa* (extended substance, matter, characterized by occupying space) and *res cogitans* (thinking substance, mind or spirit, characterized by consciousness). For Descartes, body and mind were separate entities, interacting in some mysterious way, but fundamentally distinct. This Cartesian view had an immense impact, allowing science to develop by focusing on the objective, mathematical study of the material world, free from the subjective complexities of mind and spirit, which were relegated to philosophy and theology.

Although useful in a sense for initial scientific advancement, this separation created a chasm that persists to this day, generating a sense of alienation between our inner world and the outer universe, between our search for spiritual meaning and our scientific understanding of the cosmos. We often feel like "ghosts in the machine," consciousness trapped in material bodies that seem to bear no intrinsic relation to our deepest essence.

However, science itself, by deepening its investigation into the nature of matter, began to erode the foundations of this rigid separation. As we saw earlier, twentieth-century physics revealed a surprising picture. Matter, which seemed so solid and inert, turned out to be, in essence, vibrant and dynamic energy. Atoms are vast empty spaces filled with force fields. Subatomic particles dance between wave and particle states, their properties undefined until observed. Einstein's famous equation $E=mc^2$ demonstrated the fundamental equivalence between mass and energy, showing that matter is actually highly concentrated energy.

This modern scientific view paints a portrait of matter not as something opposed to energy or dynamism, but as its condensed manifestation. Solidity is a macroscopic illusion; at the base, everything is flow, vibration, potentiality. Matter is not static "stuff," but a continuous energetic process.

This scientific understanding resonates fascinatingly with many ancient and contemporary spiritual perspectives on the nature of the physical world. In various traditions, matter is not seen as inherently evil, illusory, or separate from the divine, but rather as an expression, a manifestation, or even a "body" of spirit or universal consciousness. In some views, the material universe is God's dream, the Source's song, Shiva's dance. Matter would be spirit in its densest, most visible form. The creation of the physical world would not be an act of separation from the divine, but an act of love, of extension, where spirit ventures into form to experience itself in infinite ways.

The notion that matter is "frozen light" or "condensed spirit" appears in various mystical and esoteric schools of thought. They describe a hierarchy or spectrum of existence, where primordial energy differentiates into increasingly dense vibrational levels, from the subtlest spiritual planes to the physical plane we perceive.

We can, then, begin to envision a unifying view, a bridge over the Cartesian abyss. What if matter and spirit are not two distinct substances, but two poles of the same continuous spectrum of energy-consciousness? Matter would be energy vibrating at relatively lower frequencies, creating stable, dense patterns we perceive as physical objects. Spirit (or consciousness, life force) would be this same primordial energy vibrating at higher, subtler frequencies, manifesting as thought, feeling, intuition, life. The difference would not be of substance, but of vibrational state, of expression.

Think of water: it can exist as ice (solid, dense), as liquid (fluid), or as vapor (gaseous, invisible). These are three very different manifestations with distinct properties, yet all are fundamentally the same substance: H_2O. Similarly, matter and spirit could be different manifestations of the same underlying fundamental reality. The dense physical body would be animated and sustained by subtler energy bodies (aura, etheric body, astral body, as described in various traditions), which in turn would be expressions of an even more fundamental soul or consciousness. The ancient spiritual notion that the physical (dense) body is animated by something subtle (soul, spirit) finds a parallel in the scientific view of matter as organized and dynamic energy, not inert blocks.

Quantum physics, in particular, offers strong conceptual support for overcoming strict dualism. The aforementioned "observer effect" – the fact that the act of observing a quantum system affects its state – suggests an inescapable link between consciousness (the observer) and matter (the observed system). They cannot be fully separated in a complete description of quantum reality. Furthermore, phenomena like quantum entanglement (which we will explore later), where particles that have interacted remain instantly connected at a distance, challenge the notion of material objects as isolated and independent entities, pointing towards a fundamental holistic interconnectedness in the universe. The quantum universe doesn't look like a machine made of separate parts, but rather an indivisible network of energetic relationships, where consciousness seems to play an active role. By revealing the fluid, interconnected, and participatory nature of reality at its most fundamental level, quantum physics implicitly undermines the rigid separation between the observer (mind/spirit) and the observed (matter).

This convergence invites us to reconsider the philosophical concepts of dualism and monism. Dualism holds that there are two fundamental irreducible substances (like mind and matter). Monism, on the other hand, asserts that reality is ultimately composed of a single fundamental substance or principle. There are different forms of monism: materialistic monism (everything is matter, mind is a byproduct), idealistic monism (everything is mind/consciousness, matter is a manifestation), and neutral monism (the fundamental substance is neither matter nor mind, but something neutral that manifests as both).

The view emerging from the synthesis of modern physics and spiritual wisdom seems to point towards some form of monism. Whether it's a monism where fundamental quantum energy possesses proto-conscious properties, or a monism where Consciousness is the primordial substrate from which energy/matter emerges, the central idea is that of an underlying unity. Matter and spirit would not be enemies at war, but dance partners in the great cosmic choreography.

It is crucial to understand that recognizing this unity does not mean reducing spirituality to physics or turning science into religion. Rather, it means realizing that both may be describing facets of the same single reality, using different languages, methods, and focuses. Science seeks to understand the "how" through external observation, experimentation, and mathematical modeling. Spirituality seeks to understand the "why" and the "who" through introspection, direct experience, symbolism, and the search for meaning. They are complementary paths to knowledge. Physics can tell us about the vibrations of quantum fields, while spirituality tells us about the vibrations of love and compassion. Neuroscience can map the neural correlates of meditation, while meditative practice offers us the direct experience of inner peace. Instead of seeing them as conflicting domains, we can begin to appreciate them as different levels of description of a universe that is simultaneously physical and non-physical, energetic and conscious.

Overcoming the illusion of separation between matter and spirit is perhaps one of the most liberating steps in our journey of self-understanding. When we realize that our body is not a prison for the soul, but a sacred temple, a precious instrument for the experience and expression of consciousness in the physical world; when we understand that the material world is not an obstacle to spirit, but its visible manifestation, our relationship with ourselves and the universe transforms. We cease to feel fragmented and alienated, and begin to experience the totality of our being as physical-energetic-spiritual entities.

This integrated view empowers us to care for our bodies with more respect, to honor nature as sacred, and to seek a harmonious balance between our material needs and spiritual aspirations. It prepares us to understand how consciousness can interact with energy to shape reality, a central theme that the quantum revolution will help us explore more deeply. The dance between matter and spirit is the very dance of life, and we are all invited to participate in it with awareness and joy.

Chapter 5
The Quantum Revolution

At the end of the 19th and beginning of the 20th century, classical physics reigned supreme. Newton's laws of motion and Maxwell's theory of electromagnetism seemed to describe the universe with unquestionable precision and elegance. The cosmos was seen as a great clockwork mechanism, a deterministic system where, knowing the initial conditions of all particles, it would be possible to predict the entire future and reconstruct the entire past. Matter was solid, space and time absolute, and reality existed objectively, independent of any observer. There was a sense of completeness, that the great fundamental principles of nature had been unveiled. Only a few details remained to be refined, a few minor anomalies to be explained within this grand and seemingly unshakeable structure.

Little did the physicists of the time know that these small "clouds on the horizon," as they were called, foreshadowed a conceptual storm that would shake the very foundations of their understanding of reality, ushering in a radically new era: the quantum age.

The first significant crack in this classical edifice appeared around 1900, with the work of the German physicist Max Planck. He was trying to solve a specific problem known as the "ultraviolet catastrophe," related to the radiation emitted by heated objects (black bodies). Classical theories predicted that these objects should emit infinite amounts of energy at high frequencies (like ultraviolet light), something that clearly did not happen in practice. In an act he himself described as one of "desperation," Planck proposed a radical solution: energy was not emitted or absorbed continuously, as thought, but in discrete packets, like tiny "coins" of energy. He called these indivisible packets *quanta* (plural of *quantum*, meaning "amount" in Latin). The amount of energy in each quantum was proportional to the frequency of the radiation.

This idea of quantized, discontinuous energy went against all intuition of classical physics, where quantities were considered continuous. Planck himself initially hesitated to accept the profound implications of his own hypothesis, viewing it more as a mathematical trick than a description of physical reality. But the seed of revolution had been planted.

A few years later, in 1905, Albert Einstein boldly took the quantum idea a step further. To explain the photoelectric effect – the phenomenon where light shining on a metal can knock electrons out of it – Einstein proposed that light itself was not just a continuous wave, as believed, but also consisted of these quantized energy packets. These "light quanta" would later be called *photons*. The energy of each photon depended on its frequency (color), and only photons with sufficient energy could eject electrons from the metal, explaining why the intensity of light was not the determining factor, but rather its color. This explanation earned Einstein the Nobel Prize and provided strong confirmation of the physical reality of quanta, showing that the discontinuity introduced by Planck was not a mere trick, but a fundamental characteristic of the interaction between light and matter. Light, classically seen as a pure wave, now also revealed a particle nature.

The next crucial piece of the quantum puzzle came in 1913, with the Danish physicist Niels Bohr. He applied quantum ideas to the structure of the atom, seeking to explain why atoms were stable and why they emitted light only at specific frequencies (spectral lines). According to classical physics, electrons orbiting the nucleus should continuously radiate energy and rapidly spiral inwards, making atoms unstable. Bohr postulated that electrons could only exist in certain allowed orbits or energy levels around the nucleus, like steps on a ladder. They could not occupy the spaces in between. An electron could only "jump" from one level to another by absorbing or emitting an exact quantum of energy, corresponding to the difference between the levels, in the form of a photon of light. This model, though later refined, was remarkably successful in explaining atomic spectra and introduced quantization not only of energy but also of the structure of matter at its most fundamental level. The atom was not a miniature solar system governed by classical laws, but a quantum entity with its own strange rules.

In the following decades, especially the 1920s, an explosion of creativity from a brilliant generation of physicists – including Werner Heisenberg, Erwin

Schrödinger, Paul Dirac, Wolfgang Pauli, Max Born, and others – led to the development of the complete theory of quantum mechanics. This new theory described the behavior of matter and energy at the atomic and subatomic scale with impressive mathematical precision, but it brought with it concepts that radically challenged common sense and classical philosophy.

Strict determinism gave way to *probability*: quantum mechanics did not predict the exact outcome of a single measurement, but rather the probabilities of different possible outcomes. Nature seemed to possess an inherent element of chance or choice at its most fundamental level. *Wave-particle duality*, initially suggested for light by Einstein, was extended to matter by Louis de Broglie: particles like electrons could also behave like waves, and vice versa. And, perhaps most disturbingly, the role of the *observer* seemed crucial: the act of measuring a quantum system appeared to actively influence its state, bringing forth a reality that was previously only potential.

This avalanche of discoveries marked the end of the mechanistic worldview, of the universe as a predictable and objective clock. Fundamental reality revealed itself to be much stranger, subtler, and more interconnected than classical physics had ever imagined. The universe was not a machine made of well-defined parts, but a dynamic web of probabilistic potentials, where wave and particle were complementary aspects of the same entity, and where the separation between observer and observed was no longer absolute.

This paradigm shift was so profound that it generated intense philosophical debates among the theory's pioneers themselves. Einstein, despite his fundamental role at the beginning of the revolution, remained uncomfortable with the probabilistic and seemingly incomplete nature of quantum mechanics, famously expressing his objection that "God does not play dice." He sought a deeper, deterministic theory. Bohr, on the other hand, became the main advocate of the so-called Copenhagen Interpretation, which embraced probability, complementarity (wave and particle as necessary but mutually exclusive descriptions), and the essential role of the measurement act in defining quantum reality. Schrödinger, famous for his wave equation, illustrated the theory's paradox with his thought experiment of the cat that would be simultaneously alive and dead until the box was opened and an observation made.

These debates show that the founders of quantum physics were fully aware of the radical philosophical implications of their work, groping in the dark to understand the meaning of a world that defied human intuition.

This quantum revolution, therefore, was much more than just an advance in physics. It represented a fundamental transformation in the way science perceived the nature of reality. By breaking strict determinism, introducing probability and fundamental interconnectedness, and highlighting the enigmatic role of the observer, quantum mechanics opened conceptual doors that had been closed by the classical mechanistic view. It created a space where science could, albeit timidly at first, begin to reconsider deep questions about the nature of matter, energy, information, and even consciousness – questions that previously seemed to belong exclusively to the domain of philosophy or spirituality. Physics, which seemed to have banished mystery from the universe, now reintroduced it at its very core.

This openness, this break from strict materialism, created a potential bridge, a starting point for a new dialogue between scientific knowledge and philosophical and spiritual reflection on the ultimate nature of existence. The quantum revolution not only gave us new technologies but also offered us a new way of seeing the world and our place in it, a vision that continues to inspire and challenge us today.

Chapter 6
Wave-Particle Duality

Within the strange and fascinating world revealed by the quantum revolution, perhaps no concept challenges our intuition and language more than wave-particle duality. In the macroscopic world we inhabit, we are accustomed to a clear distinction. Things are either waves or particles. A wave, like those forming on the surface of a lake or sound waves traveling through air, is a disturbance that spreads through space, carrying energy without transporting matter in a localized way. Waves can overlap, interfere with each other (creating patterns of reinforcement or cancellation), and bend around obstacles (diffraction). A particle, on the other hand, like a billiard ball or a grain of sand, is an entity localized in space, with definite position and mass. Particles collide, bounce off, follow well-defined trajectories. In our everyday experience, these two categories seem mutually exclusive. Something cannot be simultaneously a spread-out wave and a localized particle. Or can it?

Quantum physics forces us to confront this unsettling possibility. As we saw, in the early 20th century, light, long considered a classical electromagnetic wave, began to reveal particle-like behavior through the photoelectric effect explained by Einstein – it interacted with matter as if composed of discrete energy packets, photons. This was strange enough. But the real twist came when it was discovered that the reverse was also true: entities always considered particles, like electrons, could also exhibit wave behavior. Experiments showed that beams of electrons, when passing through crystals or narrow slits, could produce patterns of diffraction and interference, phenomena characteristic of waves. It was as if electrons, under certain conditions, "forgot" their particle nature and spread out through space like waves.

This discovery, theoretically proposed by Louis de Broglie and experimentally confirmed shortly after, established the universality of wave-particle duality: not only light, but matter too, at its most fundamental level, exhibits this dual and paradoxical nature.

The most famous and perhaps most eloquent experiment illustrating this duality is the double-slit experiment. Imagine a source firing electrons, one at a time, towards a barrier with two very close slits. Behind the barrier, there is a detector screen that records where each electron arrives. If we think of electrons as tiny classical particles, we would expect each electron to pass through either one slit or the other, hitting the screen in two bands corresponding to the positions of the slits, perhaps slightly spread out due to small variations. But that's not what happens when we perform the experiment without trying to find out which slit each electron passes through. As the electrons hit the screen one by one, they gradually build up a surprising pattern:

a series of alternating bright and dark bands, known as an interference pattern. This is exactly the kind of pattern we would get if waves (like water or light waves) passed through both slits simultaneously, interfering constructively (reinforcement, bright bands) and destructively (cancellation, dark bands) with each other on the way to the screen.

The implication is astonishing: each individual electron, traveling from the source to the screen, seems to behave like a wave that passes through *both* slits at the same time and interferes with itself. How can a single particle pass through two different places simultaneously?

The strangeness increases further. Suppose we now modify the experiment by placing detectors at each slit, designed to record which slit each electron actually passes through. We want to "peek" at the electron and force it to reveal its path. The moment we do this, something dramatic happens: the interference pattern on the screen completely disappears! Instead, we get exactly the pattern we would expect for classical particles: two distinct bands behind the slits. The simple act of observing, of obtaining information about which path the electron took ("which-path information"), seems to force it to abandon its wave behavior and behave like a well-behaved particle, choosing a single slit. It's as if the electron "knew" it was being watched and decided to act accordingly. The wave nature and the particle nature seem incompatible with obtaining information about the path taken. The reality the electron manifests crucially depends on how we choose to interact with it, what kind of question we ask through our experimental setup.

Faced with this apparently insoluble paradox, Niels Bohr proposed his famous Principle of Complementarity. Bohr argued that the wave and particle descriptions are not contradictory, but *complementary*. Both are necessary for a complete understanding of quantum reality, but they apply in different, mutually exclusive experimental contexts. An experiment designed to measure wave properties (like interference in the double-slit without detectors) will reveal the wave nature. An experiment designed to measure particle properties (like the trajectory in the double-slit with detectors) will reveal the particle nature. We cannot observe both aspects simultaneously with maximum precision. They are like two faces of the same quantum coin; we can only see one face at a time, depending on how we look. The fundamental nature of the quantum entity encompasses both potentialities, and the context of measurement determines which one manifests in our observed reality. Complementarity teaches us that quantum reality transcends our classical categories and requires a subtler logic that embraces paradox.

This quantum dance between wave and particle, this complementarity of apparent opposites, resonates deeply with insights from various spiritual and philosophical traditions. The Yin and Yang symbol in Taoism, for example, represents the dynamic interplay of opposing forces (feminine/masculine, darkness/light, passive/active) which, together, form a balanced and complete whole. One does not exist without the other; they define each other and transform into each other. Wave-particle duality can be seen as a reflection of this ancient wisdom at the heart of matter: fundamental reality is not made of rigid oppositions, but of complementary polarities integrating into a greater unity. Paradox is not a sign of error, but perhaps a glimpse into the deeper nature of things.

Furthermore, wave-particle duality and the double-slit experiment strongly suggest that our perception of reality is not passive, but active. The reality that manifests seems to depend on the observer's perspective, on the type of interaction we establish with it. What we look for influences what we find. This echoes spiritual teachings emphasizing the power of the mind and intention in shaping experience. "Reality is a reflection of perception," some masters say. If we focus on divisive and limiting aspects (like observing the particle in a single slit), perhaps we experience a fragmented reality. If we open ourselves to the possibility of interconnection and potentiality (allowing the wave to manifest), perhaps we can access a more fluid and unified reality.

Finally, we can use wave-particle duality as a powerful metaphor for our own nature. Just as an electron can paradoxically be both a localized particle and a spread-out wave, perhaps we too are dual beings. We have a particle aspect: our physical body, localized in space and time, subject to the laws of biology and classical physics. But perhaps we also have a wave aspect: our consciousness, our vital energy, our spirit, which may not be strictly confined to the body's limits, which can extend, connect, vibrate in resonance with the universal field. We are, perhaps, simultaneously matter and spirit, form and potentiality, individual and part of the whole. Quantum physics, by showing us this duality at the heart of matter, invites us to recognize and embrace the complexity and richness of our own existence as "wave-particle" beings, bridges between the visible and the invisible, the finite and the infinite. Accepting this inner paradox can be a fundamental step in our journey of integration and self-knowledge.

Chapter 7
Quantum Uncertainty

The journey through the quantum territory repeatedly confronts us with the inadequacy of our classical intuition. Energy comes in discrete packets, matter and light dance between wave and particle states, and reality itself seems to respond to how we observe it. As if that weren't enough, the quantum revolution gifted us with another fundamental principle that shakes our notions of order and predictability: the Uncertainty Principle.

Formulated by the German physicist Werner Heisenberg in 1927, it establishes a fundamental and insurmountable limit to the precision with which we can simultaneously know certain properties of a quantum particle. Far from being a mere technical limitation of our measurement instruments, uncertainty reveals an intrinsic characteristic, a kind of fundamental "fuzziness" woven into the very fabric of subatomic reality.

Heisenberg's principle specifically states that there is an inverse relationship between the precision with which we can determine pairs of complementary (or conjugate) properties of a particle. The most famous pair is position and momentum (which is mass times velocity, indicating where and how fast the particle is moving). The more precisely we determine the position of a quantum particle, like an electron, the less precisely we can know its momentum, and vice versa. If we know exactly where the electron is *now*, we have a fundamental uncertainty about where it is going. If we know exactly where it is going (its momentum), we cannot know with absolute precision where it is located. There is a minimum limit to the product of the uncertainties of these two quantities, a limit imposed by nature itself, represented by Planck's constant (an extremely small but non-zero number). The same applies to other pairs of conjugate variables, such as energy and time.

Initially, Heisenberg himself tried to explain this uncertainty through a thought experiment involving a gamma-ray microscope. To "see" an electron and determine its position with high precision, one would need to use very short wavelength light (like gamma rays). However, gamma-ray photons are very energetic, and upon colliding with the electron to reveal its position, they would inevitably transfer an unpredictable amount of momentum to it, uncontrollably altering its velocity. This suggested that the very act of measuring disturbed the system fundamentally, introducing uncertainty.

This interpretation, focused on the disturbance caused by measurement, was useful, but today we understand that quantum uncertainty has an even deeper root. Uncertainty doesn't arise just because our measurements are "clumsy." It reflects an intrinsic property of the quantum nature of particles. Before a measurement, a quantum particle like an electron does not *possess* simultaneously a well-defined position and momentum in the classical sense. It exists in a state of superposition, a combination of multiple possibilities, described by the wave function. The wave function is not an image of the particle itself, but a mathematical representation of its potential state, a field of probabilities spread through space. It contains information about the probabilities of finding the particle in different positions or with different momenta, should a measurement be performed.

The inherent uncertainty expressed by Heisenberg's principle is a direct consequence of this wave-like and probabilistic nature. The particle doesn't have definite properties *until* an interaction (measurement) forces it to "choose" a particular state from the possibilities contained in its wave function, and even then, this choice respects the fundamental limit of uncertainty between conjugate properties. Quantum reality is inherently "fuzzy," potential, undefined, until the moment of interaction.

This realization dealt another devastating blow to the deterministic worldview of classical physics. If it is impossible, in principle, to know the present state of a particle (its exact position and momentum) with absolute precision, then it becomes impossible to predict its future state with absolute certainty. The laws of quantum mechanics allow us to calculate with great precision how the *probability* of finding the particle in different states evolves over time, but they cannot predict the outcome of a single specific measurement. The universe, at its most fundamental level, does not operate like a perfectly predictable clock, but rather like a cosmic game where chance and probability play an irreducible role. Nature seems to possess a spontaneity, an intrinsic freedom, that escapes rigid determinism.

This fundamental uncertainty at the base of matter resonates deeply with our experience of life and with philosophical and spiritual reflections on freedom and destiny. Human life is inherently uncertain. We make plans, but unforeseen events happen. The future unfolds in ways that often surprise us. Perhaps this uncertainty permeating our existence is not just a failure in our ability to predict or control, but a reflection of the deeper nature of a universe that is itself fluid and open.

Quantum uncertainty challenges the notion of a completely predetermined future. If not even the behavior of fundamental particles is strictly fixed, this opens conceptual space for the possibility of genuine freedom, creativity, and novelty in the universe. The age-old question of free will versus determinism gains a new perspective. If the future is not set in stone by the laws of physics, perhaps our conscious choices can truly influence the course of events. The quantum universe seems less like a machine executing a predefined program and more like a work of art in constant creation, a field of unfolding potentialities. This image of a creative and open cosmos aligns much more with spiritual visions of a living, evolving universe permeated by consciousness than with the cold, mechanical image of the past.

Even more intriguing, this "slack" in reality, this margin of indeterminacy at the quantum level, raises a fascinating question: could it be in this space of uncertainty that consciousness exerts its influence? If quantum outcomes are not always strictly determined by previous conditions, but rather chosen from a spectrum of probabilities, what or who influences this choice? Some thinkers speculate that consciousness, through focused intention or the very act of observation, could subtly act at this fundamental level, perhaps "biasing" the probabilities in favor of certain outcomes. If nature leaves a door ajar in the form of uncertainty, perhaps consciousness is the key that can turn the handle, actively participating in manifesting reality from the field of potentialities. This idea, though still speculative and outside the scientific mainstream, provides an intriguing conceptual basis for exploring phenomena like the power of intention and manifestation, which we will discuss later. It suggests that the connection between mind and matter might occur precisely in this subtle domain where classical rigidity dissolves into quantum flexibility.

Therefore, Heisenberg's Uncertainty Principle should not be seen merely as a frustrating limitation of our knowledge, but as a profound revelation about the nature of reality. It tells us that the universe, at its core, is not made of fixed certainties, but of vibrant potentialities. Uncertainty is not a defect, but perhaps the very condition for freedom, creativity, and evolution. It replaces the image of a static and predictable universe with that of a dynamic, participatory cosmos full of possibilities. By embracing uncertainty, we not only align ourselves with the most accurate description science has of the subatomic world, but we also open ourselves to a more hopeful and empowering vision of our own role within this cosmic dance of energy, consciousness, and infinite potential.

Chapter 8
The Observer

Classical physics bequeathed us the comforting image of a neutral observer, an ideal spectator who could study the universe without affecting it, like someone watching a movie on a distant screen. The laws of nature would unfold the same way, whether we were looking or not. Our measurements would be mere passive readings of a pre-existing and independent reality. However, upon diving into the depths of the quantum realm, this familiar image completely disintegrates. Quantum mechanics confronts us with one of its most baffling and profound implications: the observer is not a mere spectator, but an active participant, whose very act of observing seems to play a crucial role in determining what is real. The line between who observes and what is observed becomes surprisingly thin.

Let's recall the intriguing double-slit experiment. When we allow electrons to travel from the source to the detector screen without trying to spy on which slit they pass through, they behave like waves, creating an interference pattern suggesting that each electron passed through both slits simultaneously. However, the moment we introduce a detector to register which slit each electron traverses, the behavior changes drastically. The interference pattern disappears, and the electrons behave like well-behaved particles, passing through one slit or the other, resulting in two bands on the screen. The final outcome of the experiment fundamentally depends on *if* and *how* we choose to observe the system. Observation is not a passive act of recording what is there; it seems to actively influence what *will* be there. Observing changes the outcome.

This phenomenon, generally known as the "observer effect," is not an isolated anomaly but a central and inescapable feature of the quantum world. This leads us to the heart of the so-called "measurement problem" in quantum mechanics, an issue that has haunted physicists and philosophers for nearly a century. What, exactly, constitutes a "measurement" or an "observation" capable of transforming quantum potentialities (described by the wave function) into a definite, concrete reality? Is it any physical interaction with a macroscopic system? Is it the creation of an irreversible record of information? Or, as some have dared to suggest, does it require the involvement of a conscious mind?

Standard quantum theory describes the smooth, deterministic evolution of the wave function (potentialities) through the Schrödinger equation, but posits a second type of process, abrupt and probabilistic – the "collapse" of the wave function – which occurs during measurement, selecting a specific outcome. The exact nature of this collapse and the observer's role in it remain subjects of intense debate and interpretation.

The Copenhagen interpretation, primarily associated with Niels Bohr and Werner Heisenberg, adopts a pragmatic and somewhat radical stance. For them, before a measurement is performed, it makes no sense to talk about the properties of a quantum system as if they had a real, definite existence. The electron doesn't *have* a specific position before we measure it; it exists only as a superposition of possibilities described by the wave function. It is the act of interacting with the system through a measurement apparatus (which, in turn, must be described in classical terms) that forces nature to "choose" a specific value from the possibilities, making it real for us. Reality, in this sense, is not something we passively discover, but something we help bring into existence through our questions (experiments) and observations. The quantum world is a world of potentialities actualizing into concrete reality at the moment of observational interaction.

The renowned physicist John Archibald Wheeler took this idea to an even more provocative conclusion with his concept of a "participatory universe." Wheeler suggested that physical reality and the consciousness of observers are linked in a much deeper way than we imagine. He used the analogy of a game of "surprise twenty questions," where one person leaves the room and the others choose a word. When the person returns and starts asking yes-or-no questions, the others answer consistently, but without having chosen a specific word beforehand – the word gradually emerges from the questions asked and the answers given. Similarly, Wheeler speculated that the universe, in its early stages or even now on a quantum scale, might be undefined until acts of observation performed by conscious participants (like us) force it to assume definite forms and histories. "No property is a real (recorded) property unless it is an observed property," he stated. In this bold view, we are not mere late inhabitants of a pre-existing universe; we are essential participants in an ongoing process of co-creating reality itself. The universe becomes real, in a sense, because we observe it.

This shift in perspective – from passive spectators to active participants – represents a monumental philosophical transformation. It challenges the notion of an absolute separation between subject and object, between mind and world. If our observations help define reality, then we are intrinsically interwoven with the cosmos in a way classical physics never contemplated. We are an integral part of the system we observe, not external, isolated entities.

This idea of conscious participation in the creation of reality finds powerful echoes in numerous spiritual and metaphysical traditions. Many ancient teachings assert that our consciousness is not just a passive mirror of the world, but a creative force. "The All is Mind; The Universe is Mental," proclaims one of the Hermetic principles. "With our thoughts, we make the world," taught the Buddha. Many spiritual practices are based on the premise that our internal states – our beliefs, intentions, emotions, focuses of attention – actively shape the quality of our experience and the circumstances we encounter in life. Synchronicity, the law of attraction, the power of prayer – all these concepts point to a deep connection between our consciousness and the events of the external world.

The observer effect in quantum physics, though operating at a different level and not yet fully understood in its relation to human consciousness, provides an intriguing scientific parallel and a possible underlying mechanism for these ancient spiritual intuitions. It suggests that the boundary between the "internal" and the "external" may be more porous than we thought.

We can reflect on this with simple analogies. The old philosophical question: "If a tree falls in the forest and no one is there to hear it, does it make a sound?" Classical physics would say yes, as pressure waves are generated in the air regardless of an ear. The quantum perspective, taken to its participatory implication, might suggest that the very "quality of being sound" (the subjective experience of sound) or perhaps even the definition of the event as "tree falling producing pressure waves" only becomes concrete when there is an interaction, an observation, a record. Without an observer (be it a human ear, a microphone, or another detector), the event perhaps remains in a state of potentiality.

We invite you, the reader, to reflect: how many times have you noticed that your state of mind seems to "color" the world around you? How many times has a change in your attitude or focus seemed to coincide with a change in external circumstances? Could these experiences be glimpses of our quantum participation in reality?

If we accept, even partially, this idea of a participatory universe, it brings with it an important implication: responsibility. If we are not mere spectators, but co-creators, then the quality of our observation, the nature of our consciousness, matters. How we look at the world, the questions we ask, the intentions we hold – all these may be contributing to the reality that manifests. This echoes spiritual concepts of karmic responsibility or the ethics of cultivating positive thoughts and emotions, not just for our inner well-being, but perhaps for the good of the very fabric of reality we share.

In summary, the role of the observer in quantum mechanics serves as a fascinating bridge between the objective world of physics and the subjective world of consciousness. It shows us that observing is not a neutral act, but a dynamic interaction that participates in defining reality itself. This understanding challenges us to abandon the posture of passive victims of circumstance and to embrace our potential as conscious agents in a universe that seems to respond to our presence. Who are we, after all, if not participatory observers in this grand cosmic dance? This question impels us to investigate further the mechanism by which observation seems to transform potentiality into actuality, the mysterious process known as the collapse of the wave function.

Chapter 9
Collapse of the Wave Function

If the act of observing seems to have the power to transform the ghostly, probabilistic nature of the quantum world into the concrete reality we experience, the question inevitably arises: how exactly does this happen? What is the mechanism behind this magical transition from potentiality to actuality? Quantum mechanics describes this process through the concept of "wave function collapse" (or state vector reduction), one of the most debated and philosophically charged aspects of the entire theory. It is here, on the border between the possible and the real, that the connection between the physical universe and consciousness becomes particularly intriguing and controversial.

First, we need to deepen our understanding of the quantum state before measurement. As mentioned, a particle or quantum system, when not being observed or interacting in a way that defines its properties, exists in a state of *superposition*. This means it is not in a single defined state (like "here" or "there," "spin up" or "spin down"), but rather in a combination of all possible states simultaneously, each with a certain associated probability. The wave function is the mathematical description of this superposition, containing all the system's potentialities. It's not that the particle *is* in a definite place and we simply don't know where; the very property of having a definite position does not exist for the particle at that moment. It is, literally, in a state of multiple potentiality. Imagine a coin spinning in the air before it lands: while spinning, it is neither heads nor tails, but a potential mixture of both. Quantum superposition is an even more fundamental version of this indefiniteness.

So, what happens at the moment of measurement? According to the standard interpretation of quantum mechanics, the act of measuring a specific property of the system (its position, momentum, spin) causes an abrupt, discontinuous event: the wave function "collapses." The entire superposition of possibilities instantly disappears, and only *one* of the possible outcomes manifests as the real, observable state of the system. Which specific result will emerge in a single measurement is intrinsically probabilistic – the chances are given by the wave function itself (more specifically, by the square of its amplitude) – but once the measurement is made, the system "jumps" to that particular state. Indefiniteness gives way to definition; potentiality solidifies into actuality. The electron that was a probability cloud now has a detected position; the atom that was in a superposition of decayed and not decayed is now found in one of those two states.

To illustrate how bizarre this idea can seem, especially when extrapolated from the microscopic world to our everyday world, the physicist Erwin Schrödinger conceived his famous thought experiment of Schrödinger's Cat around 1935. Imagine a cat locked in a steel box, along with a hellish device: a Geiger counter containing a tiny amount of radioactive substance, so small that perhaps, in the course of an hour, one atom decays, but with equal probability, perhaps none decays. If an atom decays, the counter detects it and triggers a relay that releases a hammer, breaking a small flask of hydrocyanic acid, a deadly poison. If no atom decays, nothing happens, and the cat remains alive.

The question is: what is the state of the cat *before* we open the box and look, after an hour has passed? According to quantum logic, the radioactive atom, not having been observed, is in a superposition of "decayed" AND "not decayed." If the atom's state is in superposition, then the entire system coupled to it – the detector, the hammer, the poison, and consequently, the cat itself – should also be in a superposition. The cat would be simultaneously *alive AND dead* until someone opens the box and performs an observation, collapsing the wave function of the entire system into one of the two definite states: live cat or dead cat.

It's important to note that Schrödinger didn't propose this scenario because he believed macroscopic cats could actually exist in this paradoxical state. He did it to highlight what he considered an absurdity in the implications of the Copenhagen interpretation when applied to large systems. Where and how does quantum superposition end and the definite classical reality we experience begin? Schrödinger's Cat dramatizes the measurement problem and the question of wave function collapse unforgettably.

But the question persists: what, after all, causes the collapse? Here, interpretations diverge radically, and we enter territory where physics touches metaphysics.

One line of thought seeks purely physical, objective explanations for the collapse, without invoking consciousness. *Objective collapse* theories propose that the wave function collapses spontaneously under certain physical conditions, perhaps related to the size or complexity of the system, or perhaps due to new, yet undiscovered physical laws. Another popular approach is that of *environmental decoherence*. It argues that a quantum system is never truly isolated; it constantly interacts with its environment (air molecules, background photons, etc.). These interactions cause information about the system's superposition to rapidly "leak" into the environment in an entangled and irretrievable way, making the system *appear* to have collapsed to a local observer, even if the superposition still exists in the combined system (system + environment). Decoherence explains why we don't see macroscopic superpositions like Schrödinger's cat in our everyday world, but it doesn't fully solve the fundamental problem of why we get *one* specific outcome instead of another in a measurement.

Another line of interpretation, much more controversial but deeply intriguing, suggests that *consciousness* plays an essential and irreducible role in wave function collapse. Notable physicists like John von Neumann and Eugene Wigner explored this possibility.

They argued that the chain of measurement (particle -> detector -> computer -> scientist's eye -> scientist's brain) could, in principle, be described by quantum mechanics itself, remaining in superposition until it reaches the final point: the subjective consciousness of the observer. Could the conscious mind, by its nature irreducible to known physics, be the final agent that selects one possibility and makes it real? In this view, known as "Consciousness Causes Collapse" (CCC), the universe would remain in a state of multiple potentiality until a conscious mind observed it, forcing reality to define itself. Although this hypothesis is not widely accepted by the mainstream scientific community (due to the difficulty of testing it and its radical philosophical implications), it remains a fascinating possibility at the frontier between physics and philosophy of mind.

Regardless of which interpretation is correct (or if the answer is something completely different), the quantum dynamic of superposition and collapse offers a powerful metaphor for our own lives and our power of choice. We can think of our future not as a single, predetermined path, but as a vast field of potentialities, a "wave function" of life possibilities. Each crossroads, each conscious decision we make, can be seen as an act of "measurement" that "collapses" this field of potentialities into a specific trajectory. Our focused attention, our clear intentions, our deep beliefs – all these could be analogous to the act of quantum observation, selecting and actualizing certain realities over others.

If fundamental reality is made of possibilities waiting to be actualized by interaction, perhaps our consciousness is the most powerful tool we have to actively participate in this creation process. The spiritual idea that "we create our own reality" through our thoughts and choices finds a surprising echo in how quantum physics describes the emergence of concrete reality from the potential world. Wave function collapse, far from being just an abstract concept in physics, might be a glimpse into the very mechanism by which consciousness and the universe dance together in the creation of experience, moment by moment.

Chapter 10
Non-Locality

If the concepts of quantization, wave-particle duality, and uncertainty already seemed challenging to classical intuition, quantum mechanics holds an even more radical surprise, a property that seems to violate our most fundamental notions about space, time, and causality: non-locality.

The principle of locality, deeply ingrained in our everyday experience and in classical physics, states that an object can only be directly influenced by its immediate surroundings. For A to affect B, there must be some kind of physical interaction traveling from A to B through space, whether a collision, a force, or a wave, and this influence cannot travel faster than the speed of light. Quantum non-locality challenges this premise, suggesting that events in different locations can be connected instantly, correlated in a way that transcends spatial limitations, as if the distance between them simply didn't matter.

This idea was so disturbing that even Albert Einstein, one of the founding fathers of the quantum revolution, felt deeply bothered by it. In 1935, together with his colleagues Boris Podolsky and Nathan Rosen, Einstein published a famous paper presenting what became known as the EPR paradox. They imagined a scenario involving a pair of particles created together such that their states were intrinsically linked – a phenomenon we now call *quantum entanglement*. For example, we could have a pair of particles whose total spin is zero, so that if one has spin "up," the other must have spin "down," and vice versa. Quantum mechanics states that, before measurement, neither particle has a definite spin; both are in a superposition of "up" and "down." Now, imagine separating these two entangled particles by a vast distance, perhaps light-years. If we measure the spin of particle A and find it to be "up," quantum theory predicts that we will know *instantly* that the spin of particle B is "down," even if B is on the other side of the galaxy.

For Einstein, Podolsky, and Rosen, this instantaneous connection at a distance was unacceptable. It seemed to violate the cosmic speed limit established by Einstein's own theory of relativity, which states that no information or influence can travel faster than the speed of light. If measuring A truly *caused* B's state instantly, that would be "spooky action at a distance" (*spukhafte Fernwirkung*, in Einstein's famous phrase). They argued that quantum mechanics must be incomplete. There should be some "hidden variable," some predetermined property locally present in each particle from the moment of its creation, determining the measurement outcome, and the observed correlation would merely reflect these pre-existing instructions, not an instantaneous influence.

Apparently, quantum mechanics described a connection deeper than reality allowed.

For decades, the EPR paradox remained more of a philosophical debate about the interpretation of quantum mechanics than an experimentally verifiable question. This changed drastically in the 1960s when the Northern Irish physicist John Bell developed a brilliant mathematical theorem. Bell's Theorem (and its generalizations, known as Bell inequalities) provided a way to experimentally test whether reality operates according to the principle of locality and hidden variables favored by Einstein, or whether the non-local connections predicted by quantum mechanics are real. Bell showed that, under certain experimental conditions involving entangled particles, any theory based on local hidden variables would predict a maximum limit for the correlations between measurements made on the separated particles. Quantum mechanics, on the other hand, predicted stronger correlations that would violate this limit (Bell's inequalities). Nature would have to choose: either Einstein was right (locality and realism), or quantum mechanics was right (non-locality).

The experimental answer came resoundingly in the following decades, culminating in the pioneering experiments of the French physicist Alain Aspect and his team in the early 1980s. They performed sophisticated tests measuring the properties (polarization) of pairs of entangled photons sent in opposite directions to distant detectors. The results were unequivocal: the observed correlations between the photons consistently violated Bell's inequalities, exactly as predicted by quantum mechanics. Subsequent experiments, with even more advanced technologies and closing potential loopholes, have repeatedly confirmed these results. The conclusion is inescapable: Einstein's "spooky action at a distance" is real. Nature, at its most fundamental level, is non-local.

What does this mean? First, it's important to clarify what non-locality does *not* mean. Although the correlations between entangled particles are instantaneous, it is believed that they cannot be used to transmit classical information (like a message) faster than light. The outcome of each individual measurement on one of the particles remains intrinsically random; it is only in the subsequent comparison of the results from both particles that the non-local correlation is revealed. Therefore, non-locality does not seem to violate the causality principle of relativity in the sense of allowing controlled instantaneous communication.

However, the philosophical and conceptual implications of non-locality are immense. It tells us that the universe is not a collection of isolated objects interacting only with their immediate neighbors. There exists a deeper level of reality where spatial separation loses its absolute meaning. Parts of a system that interacted in the past can remain connected as a unified whole, no matter how far apart they are. Non-locality suggests an intrinsically holistic, interconnected universe, where the notion of separate parts is, in a sense, a superficial illusion. The fabric of reality seems to have hidden connections that transcend space and time as we classically conceive them.

This scientific discovery of a fundamental interconnection challenging distance resonates extraordinarily with one of the central themes of virtually all spiritual and mystical traditions of humanity: the idea of Unity, that "everything is interconnected." From the Vedic teachings on Brahman (the single underlying reality of all manifestation) and Buddhism on the interdependence of all phenomena, to the visions of Christian mystics about the Mystical Body of Christ and indigenous philosophies seeing a web of life connecting all beings, the intuitive perception of a fundamental unity beyond appearances has always been present. Quantum non-locality offers, for the first time, a scientific glimpse of this profound interconnection.

Furthermore, non-locality opens a conceptual space to consider phenomena that seem to operate beyond known physical limitations. Experiences like telepathy (apparent direct mind-to-mind communication without known sensory means), the feeling of knowing a distant loved one is in danger, or the alleged efficacy of prayer or distant healing intention – all seem less implausible in a universe that admits non-local connections. This is not to say that quantum physics *proves* these phenomena, as the mechanisms (if they exist) are unknown and likely involve the complexity of consciousness in ways we don't yet understand. However, non-locality demonstrates that nature itself operates in ways that challenge spatial separation, making the possibility of subtle connections between consciousnesses or between mind and matter at a distance somewhat less "fanciful" from a scientific standpoint.

Ultimately, quantum non-locality invites us to abandon the illusion of separateness. It shows us that the idea of being isolated individuals, confined to our bodies and separate from the rest of the universe, may be just a limited perspective. On a deeper level, perhaps we are all intrinsically connected, parts of the same indivisible whole. Recognizing this fundamental interconnection, now suggested not only by spiritual intuition but also by the discoveries of cutting-edge physics, can have profound implications for how we relate to each other and to the planet. Non-locality is a window into a universe more unified, more mysterious, and more magical than we ever imagined, a universe where distance may not be the final barrier we thought it was.

Chapter 11
Quantum Entanglement

Non-locality, that spooky connection defying distance, isn't a vague or generic property of the quantum universe. It emerges from a specific phenomenon, perhaps the most mysterious and counter-intuitive of all discovered by modern physics: quantum entanglement. If non-locality tells us *that* instantaneous connections exist, entanglement shows us *how* these connections are established and persist, revealing a level of interconnectedness in nature bordering on the inconceivable. It's a concept that led Einstein to question the completeness of quantum theory and continues to fascinate and intrigue scientists and philosophers, while deeply resonating with ancient spiritual intuitions about the fundamental unity of existence.

So, what is entanglement? Essentially, it occurs when two or more quantum particles interact in such a way that their fates become intrinsically linked, no matter how far apart they may later become. They cease to be describable as individual entities with their own independent quantum states. Instead, they become a single unified system, described by a single shared wave function. It's as if, after the initial interaction, they lose their individuality and become inseparable parts of a larger whole.

The crucial characteristic of this entangled state is the perfect and instantaneous correlation between the particles' properties. Let's revisit the example of spins. We can create pairs of particles (like electrons or photons) such that the total spin of the pair is zero. This means that if we measure the spin of one particle in a certain direction and find it "up," the spin of the other particle, measured in the same direction, will *obligatorily* be "down," and vice versa. Before the measurement, neither particle has a definite spin; both are in superposition. But their potential states are perfectly correlated by the law of conservation of total spin. When we measure one of them, forcing it to "choose" a state (e.g., "up"), the other particle, instantly and without any apparent communication, "knows" it must manifest the opposite state ("down"), even if it's light-years away. They act in unison, as if they were a single entity responding to the measurement.

To try to make this idea a bit more tangible, we can use some analogies, though none are perfect. Imagine a pair of "magic" coins that, when tossed simultaneously, are entangled such that they always land on opposite sides. If you take one coin, travel to another city, and upon arrival find it landed "heads," you instantly know the other coin, back in the original city, landed "tails." The correlation is perfect, and information about the other coin is obtained instantly upon observing yours. Another analogy, though limited because it involves predefined properties, is that of gloves: if someone puts a left glove in one box and a right glove in another, shuffles the boxes, and sends one to Tokyo and the other to São Paulo, the moment the recipient in Tokyo opens their box and finds the left glove, they instantly know the box in São Paulo contains the right glove. Quantum entanglement is similar to this correlation, but deeper, because the properties (like spin or polarization) are not defined *before* the measurement; they emerge in the act of measurement, yet still in perfect coordination between the distant particles. The "twin particles" in Alain Aspect's experiments, which confirmed non-locality, responded in unison to polarization measurements, as if linked by an invisible thread transcending space.

This connection established by entanglement seems robust and lasting. Once entangled, particles remain connected as part of a single system, no matter how much time passes or how far they travel, until a subsequent interaction (like a measurement or interaction with the environment) breaks this delicate bond. This challenges our conception of objects as independent entities existing in isolation in space. Entanglement suggests that individuality may be secondary to a more fundamental connection.

It's crucial to reiterate that, despite the instantaneity of correlations, entanglement does not seem to allow the transmission of useful information (like a coded message) faster than light. The result of a measurement on a single particle of the entangled pair remains random. Only when we compare the results obtained at both locations (which requires classical communication, limited by the speed of light) does the "magical" correlation reveal itself. Therefore, there is no violation of causality as understood in relativity. Entanglement is not about communication, but about *correlation* – an intrinsic, non-local coordination in nature's behavior, a hidden level of order operating beyond our usual notions of space and time. It's as if the entangled particles are reading the same invisible musical score, playing their notes in perfect harmony and timing, despite being on different stages and without apparent communication. Or like two hands of a perfectly synchronized cosmic clock, moving in unison despite being distinct parts.

The spiritual and philosophical resonances of entanglement are vast and profound. It offers a powerful scientific metaphor for the human experience of deep connection that seems to transcend physical distance. The intuitive feeling a mother has about her distant child, the almost telepathic connection between identical twins or soulmates, the sense of unity felt in moments of deep love or compassion – could these experiences be reflections, on a macroscopic and conscious level, of an entanglement principle operating at subtler levels of existence? If elementary particles can maintain such an intimate bond across space, perhaps our consciousnesses, emerging from this same quantum foundation, also share invisible connections we are only beginning to comprehend.

Moreover, entanglement reinforces the spiritual idea of a common origin and underlying unity. If the entire universe emerged from an extremely dense and hot initial state in the Big Bang, then all the particles that now constitute galaxies, stars, planets, and ourselves were, at some point, in intimate proximity and interaction. Could we speculate that, on some fundamental level, we still carry a trace of this primordial entanglement? Are we all, in a way, "entangled stardust," sharing invisible ties that connect us to each other and to the cosmos as a whole? This scientific perspective lends a new dimension to the ancient wisdom that "we are all one."

Quantum entanglement invites us to contemplate the nature of reality with a profound sense of awe and mystery. It suggests the universe is far more interconnected, non-local, and holistic than our everyday perception allows us to see. If particles that once interacted can remain connected forever, like invisible threads weaving the cosmic tapestry, it leads us to question the very nature of separation. Perhaps distance is an illusion, and connection is the fundamental reality. Perhaps our own consciousnesses are entangled in ways we have barely begun to imagine, participating in a vast, invisible network of information and influence that permeates the entire universe. The study of entanglement is not just about particle physics; it's about unraveling the nature of connection itself and the unity that may lie at the heart of all that exists.

Chapter 12
Cosmic Unity

As we advance in our exploration of reality through the lens of quantum physics and spirituality, the concepts we encounter – the energetic nature of matter, the participatory mystery of consciousness, the overcoming of the separation between matter and spirit, the instantaneous connections of non-locality, and the indissoluble bonds of entanglement – begin to converge towards a central image, a profound truth that resonates both in the physicists' equations and the mystics' words: Cosmic Unity. The idea that the universe, despite its apparent diversity and vastness, is fundamentally an interconnected whole, a single indivisible entity, emerges not as poetic speculation, but as an increasingly inescapable conclusion.

The notion of separation, so central to our everyday experience and classical physics, loses its solidity when confronted with quantum phenomena. If particles that have interacted can remain instantly correlated across vast distances, as entanglement demonstrates, then physical space no longer represents an absolute barrier. Distance does not break the fundamental connection. This suggests that the idea of objects as completely independent and isolated entities might be a useful approximation for the macroscopic world, but it does not reflect the deeper nature of reality. On some fundamental level, the "parts" of the universe seem to be in constant communication, responding to each other as if they were members of the same cosmic body. Spatial separation, then, becomes more an appearance than an ultimate reality.

This fundamental interconnectedness finds a powerful echo in the very history of the universe, as described by modern cosmology. The Big Bang theory tells us that the entire observable cosmos, with its billions of galaxies and trillions of stars, emerged from an initial state of unimaginable density and temperature, a point of singularity where all matter and energy were concentrated. Everything that exists today – every atom in your body, every ray of light traveling through space, every distant planet – shares this common origin. We were all, in the remote past, intimately united. Could quantum entanglement be a kind of "memory" of this primordial unity, a trace of the original connection that still persists despite the expansion of the universe? The cosmic history itself seems to whisper a narrative of fundamental unity beneath the apparent diversity.

The idea that the whole is more than the sum of its parts, and that the parts can only be understood in relation to the whole, is known as *holism*. Although science has historically been more reductionist (trying to understand systems by breaking them down into their smallest components), the holistic perspective has gained increasing relevance in various fields. In physics, thinkers like David Bohm proposed models where the universe operates holographically, with each part containing information about the whole, and where there exists an underlying "implicate order" guiding the manifestation of the explicit reality (we will explore this further). Quantum Field Theory itself describes fundamental reality not in terms of isolated particles, but of continuous, interconnected fields permeating all spacetime, with particles being mere local excitations of these fields. In biology, ecology shows us that no organism exists in isolation; every living being is part of an intricate web of relationships and interdependencies defining the ecosystem. The health of the forest depends on the interaction between trees, fungi, insects, animals, and soil. The human brain, with its capacity to generate consciousness, thought, and emotion, is another example of holism: these properties emerge from the coordinated interaction of billions of neurons, not residing in any single cell. Nature itself seems to operate according to holistic principles.

This vision of an interconnected and holistic universe, which modern science begins to outline through its discoveries and models, finds extraordinary confirmation in the perennial wisdom of humanity's spiritual and mystical traditions. Perhaps no other idea is so universally shared among diverse spiritual quests as that of fundamental Unity.

In Hinduism, *Brahman* is the Ultimate Reality, the undifferentiated Cosmic Consciousness from which everything emanates and to which everything returns; *Atman*, the individual soul, is, in essence, identical to Brahman ("Tat Tvam Asi" – Thou Art That). In

Buddhism, the concepts of *Shunyata* (emptiness) and *Pratītyasamutpāda* (dependent origination) point to the absence of inherent, separate existence; all phenomena arise in mutual interdependence, like knots in a vast net (Indra's Net). In Taoism, the *Tao* is the one, ineffable principle flowing through all nature. In Abrahamic traditions, Jewish mystics (Kabbalah), Christian mystics (like Meister Eckhart, who spoke of the "spark of the soul" being one with God), and Muslim mystics (Sufis like Rumi, who sang of the self's dissolution into the universal Beloved) described ecstatic experiences of fusion with the Divine, where the illusion of separation dissolved into an overwhelming perception of Unity. The language varies, the symbols change, but the central message is constant: we are all one.

This experience of unity is not confined to mystics of the past. A powerful contemporary example is the "Overview Effect," reported by many astronauts and cosmonauts upon observing Earth from space. Seeing our planet as a blue and white sphere, vibrant and alive, floating in the dark immensity of the cosmos, often induces a profound cognitive shift. Political borders disappear, human conflicts seem absurd, and an overwhelming sense of belonging to a single humanity and a single interconnected, fragile planetary system arises. This experience transforms the perspective of many astronauts, inspiring a deep sense of global responsibility and an almost spiritual connection to the planet and life. The Overview Effect demonstrates how a literal change in perspective can catalyze a direct perception of the unity that often escapes us in our terrestrial, fragmented view.

Thus, we witness a remarkable convergence. Cutting-edge physics, through non-locality, entanglement, and cosmological and field models, points to a universe that is fundamentally interconnected and holistic. Perennial spiritual wisdom, based on millennia of inner exploration and mystical experience, categorically affirms Unity as the ultimate truth of existence. Science, with its language of mathematics and experiment, and spirituality, with its language of intuition and direct experience, seem to be arriving, through different paths, at the same fundamental conclusion about the nature of the cosmos.

Recognizing this Cosmic Unity has transformative implications for our lives. If we are all intrinsically connected, if separation is an illusion, then how we treat others and the world around us becomes a direct reflection of our understanding of reality. Empathy, compassion, cooperation, and environmental care cease to be mere ethical ideals and become pragmatic imperatives, aligned with the fundamental structure of the universe. Harming another, ultimately, is harming oneself, as there is no truly separate "other." Cultivating love and connection becomes the most natural and intelligent way to live in a unified universe. The perception of unity dissolves fear based on the illusion of separation and opens space for trust, collaboration, and the celebration of diversity within unity.

In conclusion, Cosmic Unity emerges as a central message woven through the threads of quantum physics and the tapestry of spirituality. We are not isolated fragments floating in an indifferent void, but individualized expressions of a single interconnected, vibrant Whole. We are waves in the same cosmic ocean. Embracing this profound truth not only expands our intellectual understanding but also has the potential to heal our sense of alienation and reconnect us with our true nature and our sacred place in the grand scheme of existence. This perception of unity prepares the ground for investigating the nature of the very field that connects everything, the energetic and informational substrate from which this unity emerges.

Chapter 13
The Unified Field

The growing perception of a Cosmic Unity, supported by both the discoveries of quantum physics and millennial spiritual wisdom, leads us to a fundamental question: what is the nature of the substrate that connects everything? If the universe is not a collection of isolated parts but an interdependent and non-local whole, what constitutes this connective tissue? What is this fundamental reality from which matter, energy, and perhaps consciousness itself emerge? The answer, both at the forefront of science and at the heart of metaphysics, seems to point towards a Unified Field – a primordial field of energy and information permeating all space and time, serving as the matrix from which all existence manifests.

Since the dawn of modern physics, there has been a deep drive towards unification, a relentless quest for the "Holy Grail" of physics: a Unified Field Theory or a Theory of Everything (ToE). The goal of this quest is to find a single conceptual framework, a single set of principles, or a single fundamental entity (the Unified Field) that can cohesively describe all the forces and particles of nature. Currently, we know four fundamental forces: gravity (governing planets and galaxies), electromagnetism (responsible for light, electricity, magnetism, and chemistry), and the strong and weak nuclear forces (operating within the atomic nucleus). The search for unification aims to show that these four seemingly distinct forces are actually different aspects or manifestations of a single primordial force or field, especially under the conditions of extremely high energy that prevailed in the universe's first moments.

Albert Einstein himself dedicated the last decades of his life to this quest, trying to unify gravity (described by his General Theory of Relativity) with electromagnetism, though without complete success at the time. Today, the search continues with highly sophisticated and mathematically complex theories, such as String Theory and its extension, M-Theory. These theories postulate that the fundamental particles we observe (electrons, quarks, photons, etc.) are not dimensionless points, but tiny strings or membranes vibrating in multiple spatial dimensions (beyond the three we perceive). The different vibrational modes of these strings would correspond to the different particles and forces. Although not yet experimentally proven, these theories represent the most promising current hope for realizing Einstein's dream of a unified description of nature, suggesting that, at its most fundamental level, everything is made of the same vibrational "substance."

Regardless of the ultimate success of these specific theories, the dominant conceptual framework in current particle physics is already based on the idea of fields. Quantum Field Theory (QFT), which underlies the Standard Model of particle physics, describes reality not as a set of discrete particles moving in a void, but as a set of quantum fields permeating all spacetime. There is an electron field, a quark field, an electromagnetic field (whose excitations are photons), and so on. The particles we detect in our experiments are seen as local, quantized excitations of these underlying fields – like waves or ripples on the surface of a vast ocean. In this view, the field is the most fundamental reality, and particles are transient manifestations of its energy. The entire universe is a complex interplay of these interpenetrating and interacting quantum fields.

This field-based view of the universe has profound implications for our understanding of "empty" space itself. According to QFT, the quantum vacuum is not truly empty; it is a state of minimum energy, yet teeming with activity. Pairs of virtual particles and antiparticles constantly pop into and out of existence in quantum fluctuations, in an incessant dance governed by the Uncertainty Principle. The vacuum possesses an inherent energy, known as Zero-Point Energy, permeating the entire cosmos. Space is not a passive stage, but a dynamic medium, an energetic *plenum* serving as the substrate for the existence of fields and particles. Could this energetic quantum vacuum itself be the Unified Field, or the manifestation of an even more fundamental field?

This scientific image of an energetic and informational field underlying all reality finds extraordinary parallels in spiritual and metaphysical concepts from diverse cultures. Many traditions speak of a *Divine Matrix*, a *Mind of God*, a *Cosmic Substrate*, or a primordial *Ether* that permeates and sustains all creation. In this view, God or the Ultimate Source is not just an external creator, but the very intelligent and energetic substance of the universe. Everything that exists would be a modification, a vibration, or a thought within this omnipresent Cosmic Mind or Field. The separation between creator and creation, or between matter and spirit, dissolves in this monistic perspective.

Some contemporary thinkers have explicitly sought to connect these concepts. The philosopher of science Ervin Laszlo, for example, proposed the idea of the "Akashic Field" (or A-Field), drawing inspiration from the Sanskrit term *Akasha*, which in Vedic traditions represents the ether or primordial space, considered the repository of all memories and information in the universe (the Akashic Records). Laszlo postulates the existence of a fundamental information field in nature, a field underlying the quantum vacuum, that would connect everything non-locally and store a record of everything that has ever happened. This field would be the basis for the universe's coherence, the evolution of life, and consciousness phenomena like intuition and synchronicity. Though speculative, the Akashic Field hypothesis illustrates the attempt to build bridges between the language of field physics and esoteric wisdom about a universal information record.

We can, then, visualize the universe through a powerful metaphor: a vast, infinite ocean of intelligent energy or primordial consciousness – the Unified Field.

Everything we perceive in the physical world – galaxies, stars, planets, living beings, our own bodies and minds – would be like waves, eddies, currents, or interference patterns momentarily emerging from this fundamental ocean. We are not separate entities floating in this ocean, but manifestations of the ocean itself. Each of us is a wave, unique in its form and expression, but made of the same water as all other waves and the ocean itself in its entirety. Our individuality is real on one level, but our deepest identity lies in this underlying unity of the Field.

The idea of a Unified Field, therefore, serves as a powerful integrative concept. It represents the convergence point where the scientific quest for the fundamental unity of physical laws meets the spiritual intuition of a One Reality underlying all manifestation. This omnipresent, energetic, and potentially informational field offers a plausible basis for understanding the deep interconnection revealed by non-locality and entanglement. It might be the medium through which consciousness interacts with matter and through which information and influences propagate in ways that challenge our classical understanding. By seeing ourselves not just as connected parts *within* the universe, but as expressions *of* the very fundamental Field that *is* the universe, our sense of belonging, participation, and potential expands immensely. We are conscious waves in the vast cosmic ocean of being.

Chapter 14
Morphogenetic Fields

Our exploration of cosmic unity and the possibility of an underlying Unified Field leads us to consider whether, beyond the well-established force fields of physics (gravitational, electromagnetic, nuclear), other types of fields might exist in nature, perhaps subtler, responsible for organizing matter and transmitting information in ways we don't yet fully understand. This is a frontier where conventional science often hesitates, but where bold thinkers propose ideas that, while controversial, resonate deeply with a more holistic and interconnected view of reality.

One of the most notable and thought-provoking examples of this line of thinking is the theory of Morphogenetic Fields, proposed by the British biologist and biochemist Rupert Sheldrake. Sheldrake's central hypothesis, developed over several decades, challenges one of the central dogmas of modern biology: the idea that the form, development, and behavior of living organisms are determined exclusively by genes (DNA) and the physico-chemical interactions between their molecules.

Sheldrake argues this view is incomplete. He postulates the existence of *morphogenetic fields* (literally, "fields that generate form"), a specific type of *morphic field* (field of form or pattern). These fields would not be energy fields in the usual physical sense, but rather immaterial yet real information fields, acting as invisible blueprints or molds, guiding embryo development, tissue regeneration, crystal formation, and even organizing behaviors and habits. Each type of system in nature – whether an electron, a hydrogen atom, a water molecule, a cell, a fern plant, a bird, or a human society – would have its own characteristic morphic field, containing the collective information about its structure and behavior.

How would these fields exert their influence? Sheldrake proposes a mechanism called *morphic resonance*. The idea is that similar forms or patterns establish a connection across space and time through this resonance. Each individual organism "tunes into" the morphic field of its species, receiving information on how to develop and behave, based on the form and behavior of previous members of the same species. At the same time, each individual contributes to the collective field with its own experience, reinforcing or slightly modifying existing patterns. This creates a kind of *collective memory of nature*, where habits and forms learned or established in the past influence the present through morphic resonance. The more a pattern is repeated (e.g., the more rats learn to navigate a specific maze, or the more a chemical substance crystallizes in a certain way), the stronger its morphic field becomes, and the easier it becomes for future systems of the same type to adopt that pattern. Morphic resonance would not depend on physical proximity or known information transfer mechanisms, operating non-locally.

Sheldrake presents a series of observations and experimental evidence (much of which has generated debate and controversy in the scientific community) to support his hypothesis. One frequently cited example involves learning experiments in rats. Studies conducted over decades in different laboratories (like those of William McDougall at Harvard) seemed to indicate that successive generations of rats learned to navigate mazes or escape water tanks increasingly quickly, even when there was no possibility of genetic inheritance or direct social learning. Sheldrake interprets this as evidence of morphic resonance: the learning of earlier rats created a habit field that facilitated the learning of subsequent rats anywhere in the world. Another intriguing example is the phenomenon of crystallization: chemists often observe that new synthetic substances, initially difficult to crystallize, tend to crystallize more easily in laboratories around the world over time, as if the "information" on how to form the crystal mysteriously spreads. Sheldrake suggests the formation of the first crystal creates a new morphic field, which then facilitates the formation of similar crystals elsewhere via morphic resonance. He also applies his theory to explain complex instinctive behaviors in animals (like nest building by birds or the organization of termite colonies) and even human phenomena like collective memories, cultural archetypes, and the sensation of "phantom limbs" after amputations (the limb's morphic field would persist).

It's important to acknowledge that the theory of morphic fields and morphic resonance remains outside the dominant scientific paradigm. Critics point to the lack of conclusive and replicable experimental evidence that unequivocally isolates the effect of morphic resonance from other possible explanations (such as subtle environmental factors, sensory cues, or inadequate statistical analysis). Furthermore, the exact mechanism by which these immaterial fields would interact with physical matter and how resonance would occur across space and time remains obscure and doesn't easily fit into known physical models. For these reasons, Sheldrake's theory is often viewed with skepticism or rejected by most scientists.

However, regardless of its final scientific status, Sheldrake's theory is extremely valuable in our context as a powerful conceptual bridge between science and spirituality. His ideas, though formulated in language seeking to be scientific (fields, resonance, information), echo remarkably concepts found in deep spiritual and psychological traditions.

The idea of a collective memory accessible to all members of a species or group strongly resonates with the concept of the *Collective Unconscious* proposed by the Swiss psychologist Carl Gustav Jung. Jung postulated that, beyond the personal unconscious (derived from individual experiences), there exists a deeper layer of the psyche, shared by all humanity, containing *archetypes* – universal patterns of images and symbols inherited from our ancestors, manifesting in myths, dreams, and behaviors. Sheldrake's morphic resonance offers a hypothetical mechanism for the existence and transmission of this collective unconscious.

Similarly, the idea of morphic fields as information repositories shaping form and behavior finds a direct parallel in the esoteric notion of the *Akashic Records*. As mentioned earlier, Akasha is seen as a universal information field, a "cosmic library" containing the record of everything that has ever occurred, is occurring, and potentially will occur. Sheldrake's morphic fields could be interpreted as specific "files" within this vast Akashic field, containing the blueprints and memories of each type of system in nature.

The theory also aligns with spiritual views postulating the existence of subtle energy bodies or vibrational patterns serving as matrices for physical form and health. Thus, the theory of morphogenetic fields, even while controversial, helps us imagine *how* interconnection and information transmission beyond known physical means might operate. It provides a semi-scientific language to explore intuitive ideas about collective memory, influence at a distance, and the existence of invisible organizing principles in nature — ideas familiar and central to many spiritual worldviews. It encourages us to question whether the material universe is truly all that exists, or if it is immersed in and guided by subtle fields of information and form. In doing so, Sheldrake's theory, like other "frontier sciences," challenges the limits of the current paradigm and invites us to consider a richer, more mysterious, and more interconnected reality, where the memory of the past reverberates into the present through invisible resonant fields, weaving another thread into the complex tapestry of cosmic unity.

Chapter 15
Collective Consciousness

If information fields like morphic fields can connect members of a species through resonance, sharing habits and forms beyond direct contact, could our own minds, our consciousnesses, be interconnected in a similar way? The idea that individual consciousnesses are not isolated islands, but parts of a larger ocean, forming a Group Mind or Collective Consciousness, is another profound notion found in both cutting-edge psychology and ancient spiritual traditions. It suggests that beyond our personal experience, we participate in a shared reservoir of thoughts, feelings, and memories that unites us at subtle and often unconscious levels.

The most celebrated pioneer to scientifically explore this idea was the Swiss psychologist Carl Gustav Jung. Analyzing the dreams, myths, and symbols of his patients and various cultures worldwide, Jung noticed the surprising recurrence of certain universal themes and images that couldn't be explained solely by the individual's personal experience. This led him to postulate the existence, beyond the personal unconscious (containing our forgotten memories and repressed experiences), of a deeper, universal layer of the psyche: the *Collective Unconscious*. Jung described it as a reservoir shared by all humanity, biologically or psychically inherited, containing *archetypes* – primordial patterns of experience and behavior, such as the Hero, the Mother, the Wise Old Man, the Shadow, the Anima/Animus. These archetypes function as energetic matrices shaping our perception, emotions, and life narratives, emerging spontaneously in our dreams, fantasies, and the great cultural stories (myths, fairy tales, religions). The Collective Unconscious would be the common psychic foundation explaining why certain stories and symbols hold such universal power and why people in distant cultures can have remarkably similar dreams or visions. For Jung, consciously connecting with this deep level of the psyche was essential for the process of individuation and self-knowledge.

The idea of a shared mind can be extended beyond the inherited structures of the Jungian collective unconscious. Some thinkers propose that groups of connected people – whether a family, a community, a nation, or even all of humanity – can create or participate in a common mental field *in real time*. The French Jesuit priest and paleontologist Pierre Teilhard de Chardin, for example, introduced the concept of the *Noosphere* (from the Greek *nous*, mind). He saw evolution not just in biological terms (the Biosphere, the sphere of life), but also in terms of consciousness. The Noosphere would be a "sphere of thought," a planetary layer of collective consciousness and information emerging from the interaction of human minds, enveloping the globe. For Teilhard, evolution was heading towards an increasing complexification and unification of this Noosphere, culminating in an "Omega Point" of unified planetary consciousness.

Although these concepts might seem abstract, we can find clues and examples suggesting the operation of some form of collective consciousness or mind in our world. Consider the phenomenon of simultaneous discovery or invention: throughout history, numerous cases exist where significant scientific breakthroughs (like calculus by Newton and Leibniz) or technological innovations occurred independently and almost simultaneously in different parts of the world, by people with no contact. It's as if the idea was "ripe" in the collective field, "in the air," ready to be picked up by receptive minds.

Another example, though more anecdotal and scientifically controversial, is the so-called "Hundredth Monkey Effect," a popularized story about monkeys on Japanese islands who supposedly learned to wash sweet potatoes; once a critical number of monkeys (the "hundredth") learned the trick on one island, the behavior allegedly spread rapidly to monkeys on other islands without apparent physical contact. Even if the factual accuracy of this specific story is questionable, it captures the popular imagination because it illustrates the intriguing idea of non-local collective learning.

Perhaps more palpable is the subjective experience of connection felt during major global events. In moments of shared tragedy (like natural disasters or terrorist attacks), collective celebration (like world sporting events), or joint effort (like global peace meditations), millions of people can feel a mental and emotional union that seems to transcend borders. Does this collectively focused attention and emotion create a real, measurable field of consciousness?

This question has led to fascinating scientific investigations, such as the *Global Consciousness Project (GCP)*, initiated at Princeton University. The GCP maintains a network of Random Number Generators (RNGs) spread across the world. These electronic devices are designed to produce truly random sequences of numbers, like flipping an electronic coin millions of times. The project's hypothesis is that if a global collective consciousness exists, moments of great mental or emotional coherence shared by humanity could subtly affect the functioning of these devices, causing their outputs to deviate from expected randomness in a statistically significant way. Over more than two decades of data collection, the GCP has reported finding notable correlations between significant deviations from randomness and the occurrence of major world events that captured the attention and emotion of millions (such as 9/11, tsunamis, major elections, New Year celebrations). Although interpreting these results is complex and subject to scientific debate (as correlation does not necessarily imply direct causation), the GCP data offer an intriguing hint that collective consciousness might not just be an abstract concept, but perhaps a real force capable of subtly interacting with the physical world.

This idea of a collective mind with real power finds direct parallels in spiritual and esoteric concepts. One example is the notion of an *egregore*, often found in occult traditions. An egregore is described as an autonomous psychic entity, a collective thought-form created and sustained by the focused mental and emotional energy of a group united by a common purpose or belief (like a religious order, a secret society, a nation, or even a sports team's fans). Egregore's are believed to potentially acquire a life of their own and influence the group members and even world events, possessing a positive or negative nature depending on the intention and energy feeding them. The widespread belief in the amplified power of group prayer, collective meditation, or community rituals is also based on the idea that uniting minds and hearts focused on the same purpose generates a field of force or influence much greater than the sum of individual parts.

If the existence of a collective consciousness – be it Jung's Collective Unconscious, Teilhard's Noosphere, the field suggested by the GCP, or spiritual egregores – is real, the implications are profound. It would mean we are connected not only at a fundamental level of being (as suggested by cosmic unity) but also on a continuous mental and psychic level. Our individual thoughts, emotions, and states of consciousness wouldn't be purely private matters; they would contribute to the collective "mental atmosphere," influencing and being influenced by it. This confers upon us a shared responsibility for the quality of this collective consciousness. Mass fear, hatred, greed, and division could create toxic egregores or "pollute" the Noosphere, while mass compassion, cooperation, forgiveness, and truth-seeking could elevate and heal it.

More than that, awareness of this mental interconnection opens the possibility of moving from unconscious participants to *conscious collaborators* in the evolution of planetary consciousness. By understanding we are part of a larger mind, we can intentionally choose to align our thoughts and actions with the highest ideals of love, wisdom, and unity. We can join others in focused meditations, collaborative projects, and social movements aimed at raising the collective vibration and manifesting a more positive future for all. The idea of a collective consciousness reminds us that individual transformation and global transformation are intrinsically linked. By healing and elevating ourselves, we contribute to the healing and elevation of the whole. We are, potentially, neurons in the emerging mind of humanity, co-creating reality not just individually, but as an interconnected collective.

Chapter 16
Non-Local Mind

Our journey has led us to contemplate a fundamentally energetic universe, permeated by a mysterious consciousness, where reality seems responsive to observation and where instantaneous connections can link particles across space. We've explored the idea of information fields and the possibility of a collective consciousness uniting minds. These ideas converge on an even more radical and personal question: could *our own* individual mind operate beyond the physical limits of our brain and body? Is consciousness, this inner light animating us, strictly confined to the gray matter within our skulls, or does it possess the capacity to reach out, perceive, and perhaps even influence the world in non-local ways, transcending the barriers of physical space?

The prevailing scientific view, based on neuroscience, tends to firmly locate the mind within the brain. Consciousness is seen as a product of complex neuronal activity, and any mental experience or influence must ultimately be mediated by physical processes occurring within the body and interacting with the environment through known senses.

However, reported and investigated phenomena exist that seem to challenge this strictly local view of the mind. These phenomena, often grouped under the term "psi" (from the Greek *psyche*, mind or soul), are the subject of study for parapsychology, a research field operating at the frontiers of conventional science, systematically investigating evidence for mind-matter or mind-mind interactions that seem inexplicable by currently understood physical mechanisms.

One of the best-known psi phenomena is *telepathy*, defined as the apparent direct transfer of thoughts, feelings, or images from one mind to another, without the use of known sensory or communication channels. Although many anecdotal experiences of telepathy can be explained by coincidence, subtle cues, or logical inference, researchers have developed experimental protocols to test its existence under controlled conditions. The most famous and rigorous of these is the *Ganzfeld* experiment (German for "total field"). In this procedure, a "receiver" is placed in a state of mild sensory deprivation (with headphones emitting white noise and halved ping-pong balls over the eyes under red light) to minimize external and internal distractions. In another isolated room, a "sender" concentrates on a randomly selected image or video clip (the "target"). The receiver describes aloud any impressions, thoughts, or images that come to mind. At the end of the session, the receiver is given four options (the actual target and three decoys) and tries to identify which one best matches their impressions. Over decades and hundreds of experiments conducted in various laboratories, meta-analyses (statistical analyses combining results from multiple studies) have consistently reported a small but statistically significant hit rate, above the 25% expected by chance. Although the effect size is modest, its persistence suggests something more than luck might be involved.

Another category of psi phenomenon is *clairvoyance* or *remote viewing*, the apparent ability to obtain information about distant objects, people, or events in space, without using normal senses. Remote viewing (RV) emerged as a specific set of protocols, initially developed and researched with funding from the US government for intelligence purposes in the 1970s and 1980s, at institutions like the Stanford Research Institute (SRI). In these experiments, a "viewer," isolated and unaware of the target, attempts to describe or draw impressions of a distant geographical location, randomly selected, which might be visited by an "agent" or simply defined by coordinates. Independent judges, also unaware of the actual target, compare the viewer's descriptions with a set of possible locations (the target and some decoys) and try to find the correct match. Again, rigorous studies and meta-analyses have reported statistically significant success rates, indicating viewers could obtain accurate information about targets more often than chance would allow.

Pioneering researchers like J.B. Rhine at Duke University in the mid-20th century had already conducted extensive experiments with card guessing (testing both telepathy and clairvoyance) that also pointed to anomalous statistical effects. Contemporary researchers, such as Dean Radin, continue to investigate these phenomena with sophisticated methodologies, arguing that the cumulative weight of statistical evidence, despite being often ignored or dismissed by mainstream science, strongly suggests the reality of some form of non-local perception.

How could these phenomena occur? If the mind is strictly confined to the brain, how could it send or receive information at a distance without a known physical medium? Here, the strangeness of quantum physics, particularly non-locality and entanglement, offers an intriguing analogy and a speculative basis. If subatomic particles can remain instantly connected across space, could quantum processes occurring in the brains of two people allow their minds to become, somehow, "entangled," facilitating a telepathic connection? Could clairvoyance involve the mind non-locally accessing information directly from the fundamental quantum field, perhaps that "Akashic Field" of universal information we discussed?

It's crucial to emphasize that these are, for now, just speculative hypotheses. One of the biggest challenges is explaining how delicate quantum effects could survive and operate coherently in the brain's warm, wet, and complex environment – a problem known as the "decoherence" challenge. However, the mere proven existence of non-locality at the fundamental physical level makes the possibility of a non-local mind less *physically impossible* than previously thought. The quantum universe demonstrates that connections transcending space are part of reality.

This perspective finds deep resonance with the long-standing claims of numerous spiritual and esoteric traditions worldwide. The idea that the mind or spirit is not rigidly bound to the physical body is a recurring theme. Reports of *astral projection* or *out-of-body experiences* (OBEs), where individuals describe the sensation of their consciousness leaving the body and traveling to distant locations or even other dimensions of existence, are found in many cultures and eras. Shamanic practices often involve spiritual journeys to non-physical "worlds" to obtain healing or knowledge. Yogic texts describe *siddhis*, or psychic powers, developable through advanced spiritual practices, including the ability to perceive distant events or read minds. Although these traditions rely primarily on subjective experience and testimony, not scientific methodology, the convergence with phenomena investigated by parapsychology is notable. Psi research, with its statistical and experimental methods, could be seen as an attempt to find objective validation for capabilities humanity has intuited or experienced subjectively for millennia.

Faced with this evidence and possibilities, perhaps we need to reconsider our conception of the mind. Instead of viewing it strictly as a computational process confined to the brain, we could think of it as an *information field* – a field generated by complex brain activity, but perhaps not limited by it. This mental field could extend beyond the physical body and potentially interact with other mental fields or with a broader universal information field. In this view, phenomena like telepathy and clairvoyance would not be "violations" of physical laws, but manifestations of the properties of this non-local mental field.

Concluding that the mind may have non-local aspects is a radical step challenging the prevailing materialistic paradigm profoundly. However, the persistent anomalies reported by psi research, the possibilities opened by quantum physics, and the consistency of spiritual accounts across ages invite us to keep an open mind. If consciousness is not entirely trapped within our skulls, it fundamentally redefines who we are and how we relate to the universe. It suggests we might be connected to each other and the cosmos in ways far deeper and more interactive than conventional science usually admits. The possibility of a non-local mind is a crucial piece in the puzzle of the Quantum Soul, pointing towards a human being with a much greater reach and potential than we imagined.

Chapter 17
Beyond Space-Time

Our exploration of the non-local mind showed intriguing evidence and possibilities that consciousness may not be strictly confined to the physical space of the brain, perhaps extending and connecting in ways that defy distance. But what about the other fundamental dimension of our existence: time? Could consciousness, in its deepest nature, also transcend the barriers of the linear flow of time we experience in our daily lives? The idea that the mind might access information from the future (precognition) or the distant past (retrocognition) is even more perplexing than telepathy or spatial clairvoyance, as it seems to violate the very causal structure of the universe, where cause always precedes effect. However, persistent anecdotal reports, some lines of scientific research, and spiritual insights suggest our relationship with time might be far more complex and fluid than we imagine.

Reports of *precognition* – dreams seemingly predicting future events, sudden premonitions that come true, or an inexplicable knowledge of something yet to happen – are surprisingly common in human experience, though often dismissed as coincidence or *post hoc* memory reconstruction. Similarly, there are reports of *retrocognition*, where individuals seem to access detailed information about past events they couldn't have known through normal means, such as vivid impressions about the history of an ancient place or, most notably, cases of children claiming to remember details of past lives, extensively investigated by researchers like Dr. Ian Stevenson (a topic we'll address in more detail later). Though controversial, these reports suggest the human mind might occasionally peek beyond the boundaries of the present moment.

Attempts to capture these effects in the laboratory have produced equally intriguing and debated results. One particularly curious line of research investigates the phenomenon of *presentiment*, the idea that our body and mind can react to a future event *before* it occurs. In typical experiments, volunteers are exposed to a series of images displayed randomly on a computer, some emotionally neutral and others highly emotive (positive or negative). While viewing the images, their physiological responses are monitored (like skin conductance, heart rate, or brain activity). Several studies, conducted by researchers such as Dean Radin and Dick Bierman, have reported a surprising finding: on average, participants' physiological responses began to change a few seconds *before* the presentation of emotional images, as if the body-mind system were anticipating the emotional impact of the future stimulus. Another controversial set of studies, published by social psychologist Daryl Bem in 2011, used standard psychology protocols adapted to test "retroactive influence," finding statistical evidence that future events (like practicing word memorization *after* a memory test) could influence past performance. Although the replication of these findings is a topic of intense debate in the scientific community, they represent a direct challenge to our conventional understanding of temporal causality.

Interestingly, modern physics itself, which established the paradigm of linear causality, also offers hints that our intuitive view of time as a universal and absolute flow might be incomplete. Einstein's Theory of Relativity demonstrated that time is not absolute, but relative to the observer. The speed at which time passes depends on the observer's velocity and the strength of the gravitational field they are in. Time can dilate (pass slower) or contract (pass faster) relative to another observer. Furthermore, relativity united space and time into a single four-dimensional continuum called *spacetime*. In this spacetime block, the distinction between past, present, and future becomes less absolute, more like different locations on a map than a river flowing inexorably in one direction. The notion of a simultaneous "now" for all observers in the universe is abandoned.

Quantum mechanics also presents scenarios that seem to scramble our notion of temporal sequence. A famous example is the *delayed choice* experiment, proposed by John Wheeler. In a variation of the double-slit experiment, the decision about which property to measure – whether to observe wave behavior (interference pattern) or particle behavior (which-path information) – can be made *after* the particle (e.g., a photon) has already passed through the barrier with the slits. Surprisingly, the experiment's outcome seems to reflect the measurement choice made later. It's as if the future choice influenced the particle's past "history," determining whether it behaved as a wave or a particle when passing the slits. *"Quantum eraser"* experiments are even more sophisticated variations reinforcing this apparent retrocausality or, at least, the inadequacy of a simple linear temporal narrative for describing entangled quantum events. These experiments don't prove precognition in the psychic sense, but they demonstrate that, at the fundamental quantum level, the relationship between past, present, and future might be much subtler and more interconnected than classical physics assumed.

This view of a less rigid, linear time finds profound parallels in spiritual and mystical traditions. Many Eastern schools of thought, like Buddhism and Vedanta, describe linear time as part of *Maya*, the cosmic illusion, a construct of the mind preventing us from perceiving ultimate reality. True reality is often described as an *Eternal Now*, a timeless present containing within itself all possibilities of past and future. The goal of many contemplative practices is to transcend the linear perception of time and rest in this eternal Now, experiencing a state of pure presence and unity with the whole. Reports of deep mystical experiences often include the sensation of time dissolving, of being outside the temporal flow. Similarly, people who have undergone Near-Death Experiences (NDEs) often describe a "life review," where events from their entire existence are experienced simultaneously or non-linearly, suggesting a vantage point outside chronological time. The belief in reincarnation, present in many cultures, also implies a consciousness (soul) that persists and travels through different eras and lives, existing in a dimension transcending the time of a single physical incarnation.

Thus, both cutting-edge physics and deep spiritual experience seem to converge on the idea that our everyday perception of time as a unidirectional, inexorable arrow may be limited. Perhaps time is more like a panorama or a four-dimensional landscape, and our consciousness, under certain conditions (whether in altered states, through quantum processes in the brain, or by its intrinsic nature), can access information or perspectives transcending the linear "present moment."

This possibility invites us to reconsider our relationship with time. The present moment, the "Now," might be infinitely richer and deeper than we imagine, not just a fleeting point between a past gone and a future not yet arrived, but perhaps a portal to a broader timeless reality. If consciousness can indeed interact with reality beyond the boundaries not only of space but also of linear time, this further expands our understanding of the non-local and participatory nature of the Quantum Soul. It means our potential for perception, connection, and perhaps even influence might extend in ways we barely comprehend, suggesting an even more intimate participation in the cosmic dance unfolding not just in space, but through the very fabric of spacetime.

Chapter 18
Multidimensionality

Our journey through quantum strangeness and the depths of consciousness has led us to question the apparent limitations of space and time. We've seen how non-locality and entanglement suggest connections transcending physical distance, and how the very nature of time might be more fluid and less linear than our everyday experience indicates. Now, we dare to take a step further and ask: is the very structure of reality limited to the three spatial dimensions (length, width, height) and the single temporal dimension we perceive? Or could the cosmos be vastly more complex, housing extra dimensions or even parallel universes coexisting with ours, invisible to our senses, but perhaps accessible to consciousness or detectable by future scientific discoveries?

The idea of extra dimensions might sound like pure science fiction, but it arises surprisingly naturally in some of the most advanced theories of fundamental physics seeking to unify the laws of nature. String Theory and its successor, M-Theory, for example, which postulate that fundamental particles are actually tiny vibrating strings or membranes, mathematically require the existence of additional spatial dimensions to be consistent. Depending on the version of the theory, six, seven, or even more extra dimensions might be needed, beyond the three we know.

Where would these hidden dimensions be? The most common explanation is that they would be "compactified," meaning curled up on themselves at an incredibly small scale, much smaller than an atom (perhaps at the Planck scale, the smallest significant physical scale). Imagine a garden hose: from afar, it looks one-dimensional, just a line. But for an ant walking on it, the hose has a second circular dimension around its circumference. Similarly, the extra dimensions of string theory could be so tiny that we macroscopic beings don't perceive them directly in our daily lives, although they play a crucial role in determining the properties of particles and fundamental forces.

Another radical idea emerging from theoretical physics, this time from the interpretation of quantum mechanics itself, is that of the *Multiverse* or the *Many-Worlds Interpretation (MWI)*, proposed by Hugh Everett III in 1957. Confronted with the problem of wave function collapse (why does only one outcome manifest when many are possible?), Everett proposed an elegant, though staggering, solution: there is no collapse! Instead, *all* possibilities contained in the quantum wave function are realized, each in a separate parallel universe branching off from ours at the moment of measurement or quantum interaction. Every time a quantum event with multiple possible outcomes occurs (which happens constantly, everywhere), the universe splits into multiple universes, one for each outcome. Thus, there would exist countless parallel universes coexisting with ours, some nearly identical, others radically different, each representing a different unfolding of quantum history. Although this idea challenges common sense and is, to date, impossible to verify experimentally (as parallel universes, by definition, wouldn't interact with ours after splitting), the MWI is considered a serious and mathematically consistent interpretation of quantum mechanics by many prominent physicists, as it eliminates the need for the ad hoc collapse postulate and preserves the determinism of the Schrödinger equation at a broader level (the level of the multiverse as a whole).

What's fascinating is that these speculations from cutting-edge physics about extra dimensions and parallel universes find surprising echoes in cosmologies and descriptions of reality found in numerous spiritual, esoteric, and mystical traditions worldwide. Long before String Theory or the MWI, various cultures described the cosmos not as a single, monolithic entity, but as a multi-layered structure, composed of different *planes of existence*, *spheres*, or *dimensions*. Theosophical, Gnostic, Kabbalistic, and other mystery schools often describe a hierarchy of planes interpenetrating the physical world, such as the etheric plane (associated with vital energy), the astral plane (associated with emotions and dreams, often seen as the realm inhabited by souls after death), the mental plane (associated with thoughts and ideas), and even higher spiritual planes (causal, buddhic, atmic). Each plane would be characterized by a subtler "vibration" or "substance" than the plane below and inhabited by beings or consciousnesses appropriate to that level of reality. The idea is that the physical reality we perceive is only the densest manifestation of a much vast_er_ and more complex cosmic structure. These planes wouldn't necessarily be "above" or "below" in physical space, but would interpenetrate our reality, existing in different "dimensions" or vibrational "frequencies."

The alignment between these spiritual cosmologies and scientific speculations is remarkable. Could the "astral plane" described by mystics and astral projectors somehow be analogous to one of these extra dimensions postulated by physics, or perhaps a parallel universe close to ours, accessible to consciousness under certain conditions? Could the "beings of light" or "spirit guides" reported in near-death or mediumistic experiences be inhabitants of these other dimensions or planes of existence? While drawing direct equivalences is premature and perhaps naive, the conceptual resonance is undeniable and suggests that both science and spirituality might be groping, in different ways, towards the same truth of a multidimensional reality.

Beyond cosmological descriptions, there are also reports of subjective experiences seemingly corroborating the idea of accessing other dimensions. Individuals who have undergone profound Near-Death Experiences (NDEs) often describe leaving the physical body and entering realms of light, peace, and knowledge that seem radically different from our three-dimensional reality, sometimes encountering deceased relatives or luminous beings. Practitioners of astral projection or out-of-body travel claim to be able to consciously explore these non-physical realms. Mediums and channelers allege communication with intelligences or consciousnesses residing on these other planes. Even experiences like intense lucid dreams or visionary states induced by deep meditation or psychoactive substances can sometimes give the vivid sensation of entering coherent and complex alternative realities. Although interpreting these experiences is complex (potentially involving cerebral, psychological, and perhaps genuinely transcendental processes), they contribute to the sense that the reality we perceive might just be the tip of the cosmic iceberg.

The possibility of multidimensionality invites profound humility and open-mindedness. Our senses evolved to help us survive in a specific three-dimensional physical environment, and our current scientific instruments are also limited in their ability to probe reality. Just because we don't directly see, hear, or measure other dimensions or universes doesn't mean they don't exist. Mathematics, the fundamental language of physics, allows and even suggests the existence of spaces with many more dimensions than the three we experience. Spiritual traditions, based on inner exploration of consciousness, consistently describe a multi-layered reality. Perhaps science and spirituality are offering us complementary glimpses of a cosmos whose vastness and complexity surpass our current imagination.

Therefore, the idea of multidimensionality, whether in the form of extra spatial dimensions, parallel universes, or vibrational spiritual planes, radically expands our concept of reality. It suggests the visible universe might be just one membrane or slice within a much larger "Multiverse" or "Omniverse." This perspective has profound implications for our understanding of the nature of consciousness, the possibility of life after death, and the journey of the Quantum Soul through different levels of existence. It reminds us we are citizens of a cosmos potentially infinite in its creativity and mystery, inviting us to explore not only the outer universe but also the inner dimensions of our own consciousness, which might be the key to accessing these other realities.

Chapter 19
Holographic Universe

As we delve deeper into the interconnected and multidimensional nature of reality suggested by quantum physics and the exploration of consciousness, we encounter an even more radical and unifying idea: the Holographic Universe hypothesis. This fascinating perspective proposes that the universe, in its entirety or in fundamental aspects of its functioning, might be structured like a gigantic hologram. In a hologram, each individual part contains information about the whole, in a way that challenges our usual understanding of space and information. If this hypothesis is correct, it would have profound implications for our understanding of reality, consciousness, and our own nature intrinsically connected to the cosmos.

To grasp the idea, we first need to understand what a hologram is. Unlike a regular photograph, which captures a two-dimensional image where each point on the film corresponds to a point in the scene, a hologram is a three-dimensional recording created by the interference of laser light beams. A laser beam is split: one part illuminates the object to be recorded, and the light reflected from it is directed onto a special photographic plate; the other part of the beam (the reference beam) is directed straight onto the same plate. The complex interference pattern between these two beams is what gets recorded on the holographic plate. When this plate is later illuminated by a laser beam similar to the original reference beam, it recreates the object's original light field, generating a three-dimensional image that appears to float in space, complete with depth and parallax (the image changes as the observer moves their head).

The most surprising property of the hologram, however, is the *non-locality of information*: if you break the holographic plate into pieces, each individual piece, when illuminated, will be able to reconstruct the entire three-dimensional image (though with less detail or clarity than the complete hologram). Information about the whole is somehow distributed throughout the entire extent of the film.

This unique property of holograms inspired two prominent thinkers, working independently in different fields, to propose that the universe or the mind might operate according to holographic principles.

Physicist David Bohm, a collaborator of Einstein and one of the deepest thinkers on the foundations of quantum mechanics, proposed a view of reality based on two orders: the *explicate order*, which is the manifest world of separate forms, objects, and events we perceive in space and time; and the *implicate order*, a deeper, unmanifest level of reality where everything is interconnected and enfolded. For Bohm, the explicate order continuously unfolds from the implicate order, and the implicate order is present everywhere. He used the analogy of a hologram to describe this relationship: just as the 3D image (explicate order) emerges from the holographic plate (containing the enfolded information of the implicate order), the manifest universe emerges from a more fundamental background where everything is interconnected. Apparent separation in the explicate order would be an illusion, as in the implicate order, everything is one.

Concurrently, neuroscientist Karl Pribram at Stanford University was struggling to understand how the brain stores memories. He noted that memories don't seem localized in specific brain areas; extensive brain damage might impair recall ability but rarely erases specific memories completely. This led him to propose the *holonomic brain model*, suggesting memories are not stored in individual neurons but distributed throughout the brain (or large regions of it) as patterns of neural interference, analogous to a hologram. Perception could also operate holographically, with the brain processing frequencies and patterns from the external world and transforming them into our concrete experience. When Bohm and Pribram learned of each other's work, they recognized the profound synergy between their ideas, leading to the development of the "Bohm-Pribram Holographic Universe" model, suggesting the brain operates holographically to access a reality that is itself holographic in its fundamental nature.

More recently, and independently, the idea of a holographic principle emerged from a very different field of theoretical physics: the study of black holes and the search for a quantum theory of gravity, especially within the context of String Theory. Physicists like Gerard 't Hooft and Leonard Susskind discovered that the maximum amount of information that can be contained within a region of space is not proportional to its volume (as one might expect), but to the area of its boundary surface. This is particularly evident in black holes, where it's postulated that all information about what fell into them is somehow encoded in quantum fluctuations on the surface of the event horizon (the black hole's point of no return). This surprising relationship between information, volume, and area led to the formulation of the *Holographic Principle*: the idea that the complete description of a three-dimensional physical system might be equivalent to a quantum theory operating only on the two-dimensional boundary of that system. In other words, our familiar three-dimensional reality could be, in a fundamental sense, a holographic projection of information encoded on a distant surface, perhaps at the edge of the observable universe. Although still an active and speculative area of research, the Holographic Principle has become an influential idea in theoretical physics, suggesting the holographic nature of reality might be more than just a metaphor.

    The idea of a holographic universe, where the whole is contained in each part, resonates extraordinarily with fundamental principles found in ancient esoteric and spiritual wisdom traditions. The Hermetic maxim "As above, so below; as below, so above," found in the Emerald Tablet, succinctly expresses this correspondence between different levels of reality. The concept of *microcosm and macrocosm*, present in many cultures, teaches that the human being (the microcosm) is a miniature reflection of the entire universe (the macrocosm), containing within itself all the elements and laws governing the cosmos. "Know thyself and thou shalt know the universe and the gods," read the inscription at the Oracle of Delphi. If the universe operates holographically, then this correspondence is not merely symbolic; each part literally contains or reflects the information of the whole. The spiritual idea of the "divine spark," the "Atman," or the "Buddha nature" present in every sentient being finds a plausible model in the hologram: the essence of Ultimate Reality (God, Brahman, Cosmic Consciousness) is not just "out there," but also enfolded within each individual consciousness. We are like drops of water, each reflecting within itself the entire image of the vast ocean.

Fractal geometry, discovered by modern mathematics but intuitively present in art and nature, offers another beautiful analogy for the holographic principle. Fractals are complex patterns exhibiting *self-similarity* – the same basic shape repeats at smaller and smaller scales. Think of a snowflake, a fern leaf, or a coastline: zooming in on a small part reveals patterns similar to the overall pattern. The structure of the whole is mirrored in its parts. This "holographic" characteristic of fractals suggests nature might employ similar design principles, where complexity emerges from the repetition of simple patterns at different scales, reflecting an underlying unity.

Subjective experience can also give us glimpses of this holographic nature. In states of deep meditation, peak experiences, or moments of profound connection with nature, some people report a dissolution of boundaries between self and world, a sense of unity where the entire universe seems contained within their own consciousness, or where they perceive luminous, interconnected patterns permeating everything. These experiences, often difficult to describe in ordinary language, can be interpreted as direct perceptions of the implicate order or the holographic nature of reality, where separation is transcended and fundamental unity is revealed.

The Holographic Universe hypothesis, therefore, offers a powerful and unifying conceptual framework intertwining frontier physics, neuroscience, and spiritual wisdom. It suggests a reality where information is fundamental and non-locally distributed, where each part contains the essence of the whole, and where we are all intrinsically connected, not just by external threads, but by being, in ourselves, reflections and carriers of the entire cosmos. This vision inspires a profound sense of unity and belonging, and reminds us that the journey to understand the universe and the journey to understand ourselves are, ultimately, the same quest for the totality residing both outside and within us.

Chapter 20
Quantum Consciousness

Our journey thus far has revealed a strange and wonderful quantum universe, a realm of energy, potentiality, interconnectedness, and participation that challenges our classical intuition. We've explored how these principles might offer new perspectives on the nature of reality, the relationship between matter and spirit, and even the possibility of a collective or non-local mind. Now, we arrive at the most intimate and perhaps most crucial point of convergence: the attempt to directly apply the principles of quantum physics to unravel the greatest mystery of all – the nature of consciousness itself. Could quantum phenomena be not just an analogy or a backdrop for consciousness, but the very mechanism by which it arises and operates? Is the key to the "hard problem" of subjective experience hidden in the laws governing the subatomic world?

The traditional view in neuroscience, while acknowledging the immense complexity of the brain, tends to treat it as a biological machine operating according to the principles of classical physics and chemistry. Neurons fire electrical signals, neurotransmitters cross synapses – all would ultimately be a highly sophisticated, albeit wet and biological, computational process. Consciousness would be an emergent property of this classical computation, software running on neural hardware.

However, as we've seen, explaining *how* and *why* this classical computation should give rise to subjective experience, to inner "feeling," remains a profound challenge. This has led some scientists and philosophers to question whether the classical model is sufficient. What if the brain is not just a classical computer, but also a special kind of *quantum computer*, harnessing the subtle and powerful effects of the subatomic world to generate consciousness itself?

One of the most detailed and debated theories proposing a quantum basis for consciousness is the Orch OR (Orchestrated Objective Reduction) theory, developed by mathematical physicist Sir Roger Penrose and anesthesiologist Stuart Hameroff. The theory suggests the seat of consciousness lies not primarily in the synapses between neurons, but in much smaller structures within them: the *microtubules*. Microtubules are components of the cell cytoskeleton, hollow protein cylinders playing roles in cell structure, transport, and division. Hameroff proposed that the regular, almost crystalline structure of microtubules could allow them to sustain states of *quantum coherence* – where multiple components (tubulin protein subunits within microtubules) vibrate in unison, maintaining a quantum superposition state for long enough, shielded from the brain's noisy environment.

Penrose, in turn, proposed a physical mechanism for wave function collapse, called *Objective Reduction*

(OR). He argued that quantum superposition cannot grow indefinitely, especially for larger systems, as it would create a superposition of spacetime itself (due to general relativity); when this superposition reaches a certain threshold of gravitational instability (at the Planck scale), it would collapse spontaneously – an *objective* reduction, not dependent on an external observer. In the Orch OR theory, these Objective Reduction events occurring in an *orchestrated* manner within brain microtubules would correspond to the discrete moments of conscious experience, the "frames" of our perception. Consciousness, therefore, would not be a continuous computational process, but a sequence of discrete quantum events occurring in the brain's fine structure. The brain would be a quantum machine tuned to generate moments of proto-consciousness that integrate into our rich, continuous experience.

Other researchers have proposed different approaches connecting quantum physics to the mind. Physicist Henry Stapp, for example, strongly influenced by John von Neumann's ideas, suggests that the conscious mind (viewed perhaps as an entity distinct from the physical brain, though interacting with it) actively utilizes quantum effects in the brain to exert its will. The mind could use the so-called *Quantum Zeno Effect* (the idea that repeatedly observing a quantum system can "freeze" it in one state, preventing its evolution – like the watched pot that never boils) to maintain certain patterns of neural activity (representing intentions or thoughts) in a state of potential superposition for a period. When the conscious mind decides to act, it would release this "quantum attention," allowing the wave function to collapse and trigger the corresponding neural action in the brain. In this view, consciousness doesn't emerge from the quantum brain, but rather *uses* the brain's quantum physics as an interface to interact with the physical world.

A philosophical perspective gaining renewed interest and potentially related to a quantum view is *panpsychism*. Panpsychism challenges the idea that consciousness is an exclusive property of complex systems like brains. Instead, it proposes that consciousness (or some rudimentary form of proto-consciousness) is a *fundamental* and ubiquitous property of matter, much like mass or electric charge. Every elementary particle, every quantum field, would possess a minimal degree of subjective experience. The complex consciousness we experience as humans wouldn't emerge from nothing out of purely non-conscious matter, but would be built up from the combination and organization of these fundamental conscious building blocks. Theories like Giulio Tononi's Integrated Information Theory (IIT), which seeks to measure the amount of consciousness in a system based on its capacity to integrate information, can be seen as compatible with a form of panpsychism. If consciousness is fundamental in nature, the "hard problem" dissolves – the question isn't how consciousness arises from matter, but how fundamental consciousness organizes into more complex forms.

Going even further, some physicists, like Amit Goswami, advocate a form of *monistic idealism* based on the interpretation of quantum mechanics. For quantum idealism, *consciousness* is the primary and fundamental reality, the "ground of all being." The material universe, including space, time, and matter, does not exist independently of consciousness, but rather emerges *from* or *within* it. Quantum mechanics, with its central role for the observer, non-locality, and probabilistic nature, is seen as the physics describing how the One, fundamental Consciousness manifests as the multiple, apparently material world we perceive. Wave function collapse would be the act by which Consciousness chooses one possibility and makes it real within itself. In this view, matter doesn't produce consciousness; Consciousness produces (or manifests as) matter.

What is remarkable about all these diverse approaches – whether Orch OR locating consciousness in quantum processes in microtubules, Stapp postulating the mind using cerebral quantum effects, panpsychism making consciousness a fundamental property of matter, or quantum idealism seeing consciousness as the very basis of reality – is the convergence towards the idea that consciousness and the physical world (particularly the quantum one) are intrinsically intertwined. Science, in its quest to explain the mind, is being led to seriously consider that consciousness is not a secondary epiphenomenon, but perhaps a fundamental, maybe even primary, aspect of the universe's structure.

This trend represents an extraordinary rapprochement with spiritual worldviews that, in diverse ways, have always affirmed the primacy or fundamentality of Consciousness, Spirit, or the Cosmic Mind. The idea of an omnipresent Spirit, of a Consciousness that is the source and substance of all creation, finds an unexpected echo in these frontier scientific theories. Science, with its rigorous language and empirical methodology, seems to be rediscovering, from within, the possibility that the universe is far more mental and conscious than the materialistic paradigm allowed us to imagine.

Although none of these quantum theories of consciousness are yet proven or universally accepted, the mere fact they are being proposed and seriously debated by renowned scientists signals a potentially seismic shift in our understanding. They suggest the "Quantum Soul" might not be just a poetic metaphor, but perhaps a more literal description of our nature as conscious beings immersed in a participatory quantum universe. The search for a quantum theory of consciousness is the search for the very interface between spirit and matter, promising not only to revolutionize science but also to validate and deepen our spiritual understanding of who we are and our place in the cosmos.

Chapter 21
Consciousness Beyond the Body

We now arrive at one of the deepest and most universally human questions: what happens to us when we die? Does the flame of consciousness, this experience of being that accompanies us throughout life, simply extinguish when the brain ceases to function? Or is there something within us – a soul, a spirit, consciousness itself – that persists beyond the death of the physical body? For millennia, religions and spiritual traditions worldwide have offered affirmative answers, consoling and guiding humanity with narratives about the soul's immortality and the existence of life after death. Modern science, for the most part, has adopted a more skeptical stance, tending to view consciousness as an exclusive product of brain activity and therefore destined to cease with the end of that activity. However, in recent decades, certain lines of scientific investigation and reports of anomalous experiences have begun to challenge this purely materialistic view, opening space for the possibility that consciousness may indeed transcend the limits of the physical body.

The standard materialistic view is straightforward: the mind is what the brain does. All our thoughts, feelings, memories, and the very sense of being are generated by the complex network of neurons and biochemical processes in our brain. When the brain suffers irreversible damage and dies, the physical basis of consciousness disappears, and therefore, consciousness must also cease. Any report of conscious experiences seemingly occurring outside a functioning brain would, in this view, be attributed to hallucinations, residual brain processes, memory distortions, or psychological constructions. This perspective seems logical, given the strong correlation we observe between brain health and mental states.

However, a growing body of empirical evidence challenges this apparently inevitable conclusion. *Near-Death Experiences (NDEs)* represent perhaps the most significant challenge. These are vivid and often transformative accounts by people who were declared clinically dead (usually due to cardiac arrest, when the heart stops beating and detectable brain activity ceases or is severely compromised) and were subsequently resuscitated. Despite being unconscious from a medical standpoint, many of these individuals describe lucid, structured, and profoundly meaningful experiences.

The reports often share remarkable common elements, regardless of the individual's culture, age, or prior religious beliefs: an overwhelming sense of peace and well-being; the sensation of leaving the physical body and observing the scene (often their own body being resuscitated) from an external perspective (autoscopy); the feeling of moving through a dark tunnel towards a bright, welcoming light; encountering deceased loved ones or beings perceived as spiritual or divine; a panoramic, non-judgmental review of one's life; and often, a reluctance to return to the physical body, followed by a profound transformation in values and life perspective after the experience.

From a scientific viewpoint, the most intriguing aspect of NDEs are cases of *veridical perception.* In these cases, individuals report observing, while out of body and clinically dead, specific details of events occurring in the operating room, other hospital rooms, or even outside the hospital – details they could not have perceived through normal senses or known by other means. For example, accurate descriptions of medical procedures, conversations among medical staff, the appearance of specific surgical instruments, or events involving family members in distant waiting rooms. Researchers like Dr. Raymond Moody (who popularized the term NDE in his book "Life After Life"), Dutch cardiologist Dr. Pim van Lommel, and psychiatrists like Dr. Bruce Greyson and Dr. Sam Parnia (with his AWARE studies, attempting to place visual targets in locations visible only from an elevated perspective in resuscitation rooms) have documented and analyzed these cases. The ability to have clear, organized, and sometimes veridical perceptions during a period of severe brain dysfunction or absence of detectable brain activity presents a profound enigma for the model equating consciousness exclusively with normal brain function.

Another line of research suggesting the continuity of consciousness beyond a single physical life is the investigation of *spontaneous past-life memories* in young children. The pioneering work of Dr. Ian Stevenson, a psychiatrist at the University of Virginia, continued by colleagues like Dr. Jim Tucker, has meticulously documented thousands of cases worldwide. Typically, children between two and five years old spontaneously begin talking about a previous life, providing surprisingly specific details about names of people and places, family relationships, occupation, and often, the manner of death in the past life (frequently violent or premature). Stevenson's team then sought to locate a deceased person whose life details matched the child's statements. In a significant number of cases, a match was found, and many details provided by the child were objectively verified, even those seeming obscure or unknown to the child's current family. Furthermore, in some cases, children exhibited unusual behaviors, phobias, or affinities seemingly related to the alleged past life, or even possessed birthmarks or congenital defects corresponding to fatal wounds (like gunshot or stab wounds) on the deceased person's body. Although alternative explanations like fraud (rarely found), cryptomnesia (hidden memory of normally acquired information), or cultural influence need consideration, Stevenson concluded that, in the strongest cases, the hypothesis of reincarnation (the survival of personality or consciousness in some form and its rebirth in a new body) appeared to be the most plausible explanation.

Faced with this challenging empirical data, some scientists have begun to speculate whether quantum physics itself might offer some perspective on the possibility of consciousness survival. As we've seen, information, in some physics contexts (like black hole thermodynamics), is considered a fundamental entity that perhaps cannot be destroyed. Could consciousness, as an extremely complex form of organized information, also be subject to some kind of conservation principle? Stuart Hameroff, proponent of the Orch OR theory of quantum consciousness in microtubules, speculated that the quantum information constituting consciousness might, at the moment of clinical death, not be destroyed, but rather "leak" or dissipate into the fundamental quantum field of the universe. If resuscitation occurs, this quantum information could theoretically return to the brain microtubules, explaining the continuity of consciousness and memories reported in NDEs. It's important to reiterate that this is a highly speculative hypothesis, based on another speculative theory (Orch OR), but it illustrates an attempt to think about survival within a potentially physical framework. Alternatively, if we adopt an idealist or panpsychist view (as discussed in the previous chapter), where consciousness is fundamental and not a product of matter, then brain death would merely be the end of its particular physical manifestation, not the end of consciousness itself, which would continue to exist in the underlying universal field of consciousness.

Naturally, these lines of evidence and scientific speculation resonate directly with the fundamental beliefs of most spiritual traditions about the *immortal soul*. The idea that our conscious essence survives the death of the physical body is a pillar of hope and meaning for billions. NDEs, with their descriptions of realms of light and encounters with spiritual beings, seem to offer glimpses consistent with many traditional views of the "afterlife." Research on reincarnation directly supports the belief in the soul's continuity through multiple lives. Concepts like the *perispirit* in Spiritism – a subtle, semi-material body enveloping the soul, serving as a mold for the physical body, persisting after death, and carrying identity and memories – offer an explanatory model for how consciousness might perceive the environment during an out-of-body NDE or how memories could be transported to a new incarnation.

The question of consciousness survival after death undoubtedly remains one of the greatest mysteries of human existence. Science does not yet have a definitive answer. However, the accumulated evidence from rigorous study of NDEs and suggestive cases of reincarnation, combined with the conceptual possibilities opened by quantum physics and philosophy of mind, seriously challenge the simplistic view that consciousness is merely a ghost in the machine that vanishes when the machine stops. These clues suggest consciousness might be more fundamental, more resilient, and less dependent on the physical brain than the materialistic paradigm assumes. They offer not irrefutable proof, but a rational basis for hope and open-mindedness regarding the possibility that our conscious journey continues beyond the horizon of physical death. This possibility is central to the very idea of a Quantum Soul – an entity of consciousness and information that may indeed transcend the limitations of body and linear time.

Chapter 22
The Power of Intention

Our exploration of the quantum universe has revealed a surprisingly participatory reality, where the act of observing seems to influence what is observed, where non-local connections weave an invisible web across space, and where consciousness itself may transcend the limits of body and time. If consciousness is so intrinsically interwoven with the fabric of the cosmos, a question of immense practical and spiritual potential arises: can we go beyond mere passive observation or anomalous perception? Could our directed thoughts, our focused wills – our *intentions* – have the power to actively influence the physical reality around us? The idea that mind can affect matter, known as psychokinesis (PK) or telekinesis, has long been relegated to the realm of fantasy or pseudoscience, but frontier research and well-established phenomena like the placebo effect suggest the power of intention might be real and measurable.

When we speak of "intention," we refer to something more than a passing thought or vague wish. Intention implies a conscious directing of the mind, a sustained mental focus imbued with purpose, will, and often, feeling. It's the difference between passively noticing a cloud and actively willing it to dissipate, focusing mental energy on that goal. While the "observer effect" in quantum physics seems to occur even with passive observation (though the definition of "observation" is complex), investigation into the power of intention explicitly focuses on the mind's ability to *direct* an influence onto physical or biological systems.

For decades, researchers in parapsychology and anomalous psychology have attempted to detect and measure these subtle mind-over-matter effects in controlled laboratory settings, primarily focusing on so-called *micro-psychokinesis* (micro-PK) – mental influence on probabilistic or delicate systems at a microscopic scale. One of the best-known and most controversial research programs in this area was conducted at Princeton University's PEAR (Princeton Engineering Anomalies Research) laboratory, under the direction of Robert Jahn and Brenda Dunne, for nearly thirty years. In their most famous experiments, volunteers (called "operators") were instructed to focus their intention to influence the output of Random Number Generators (RNGs). These electronic devices are designed to produce truly random sequences of bits (equivalent to flipping an electronic coin millions of times per second). Operators attempted to make the RNG output deviate from the expected chance (50% 0s and 50% 1s), either towards more 1s (High), more 0s (Low), or simply to maintain the baseline (Baseline). Over hundreds of experiments with dozens of operators, the PEAR lab reported accumulating data showing small but statistically significant and consistent deviations in the direction of the operator's intention. Curiously, they also observed individual "signatures" – each operator seemed to produce a characteristic pattern of deviation, regardless of the intention (High or Low). Although PEAR's methodology and statistical interpretation have been intensely debated in the scientific community, their results remain a body of anomalous data challenging a purely chance explanation. Similar RNG research conducted by other labs worldwide has also reported small but significant effects, suggesting focused human intention might indeed exert a subtle influence on random events.

Outside the rigorous but limited environment of RNGs, other researchers have explored the influence of intention on more complex biological or physical systems. An example that gained immense popularity, though lacking rigorous scientific validation, is the work of Japan's Masaru Emoto with water crystals. Emoto claimed water's molecular structure could be affected by human intention. He exposed water samples to different stimuli – written words (like "love and gratitude" or "hate"), music, prayers, or directed thoughts – then rapidly froze small drops of this water, photographing the resulting ice crystals under a microscope. His widely circulated photographs showed water exposed to "positive" intentions tended to form beautiful, complex, symmetrical ice crystals, resembling perfect snowflakes, while water exposed to "negative" intentions formed ugly, distorted, chaotic structures, or failed to form crystals at all. It's crucial to note Emoto's work was severely criticized by the scientific community for serious methodological flaws (lack of adequate controls, subjective image selection, lack of independent replication). Therefore, his conclusions cannot be considered scientifically proven. However, the immense popular resonance of his images attests to how deeply the idea that our thoughts and emotions can affect matter resonates with human intuition. It serves, at the very least, as a powerful visual metaphor for the principle of intention.

If the mind's influence on external systems like RNGs or (potentially) water remains controversial, there is one domain where the power of mind over matter is scientifically undeniable: our own bodies. The *placebo effect* is a robust and well-documented example of this mind-body connection. In clinical studies, it's consistently observed that a significant percentage of patients receiving an inert treatment (like a sugar pill or saline injection) but believing they are receiving a real drug, experience real, measurable improvements in their symptoms. This positive belief and expectation can trigger concrete physiological responses: release of endorphins (the body's natural painkillers), modulation of the immune system, changes in brain activity and neurotransmitter levels, and even, in some cases, tumor shrinkage or cure of objective conditions. The placebo effect is not "just psychological"; it's a clear demonstration that a mental state (belief, expectation) can produce tangible physical changes in the body. The inverse phenomenon, the *nocebo effect*, where negative expectations can lead to worse health outcomes, is also real. The placebo/nocebo effect provides irrefutable scientific proof that the mind has power over matter – at least, the matter of our own bodies.

How, then, might intention work, especially on external systems? The exact mechanisms remain unknown and speculative. Could focused intention act at the quantum level, subtly influencing the inherent probabilities of random systems, perhaps "guiding" the wave function collapse in a preferred direction? Could intention imprint information onto underlying fields (the quantum vacuum, morphic fields, the Akashic Field), which then interact with matter? Or could the non-local mind directly interact with distant systems through connections we don't yet understand? These are all intriguing possibilities emerging from the quantum and holistic worldview we are constructing, but they require much more investigation.

Regardless of the exact mechanism, the idea of the power of intention is deeply rooted in universal human practices and spiritual teachings. *Prayer*, in many traditions, is seen not just as a request to a deity, but as an act of directing focused mental and spiritual energy towards healing, protection, or manifesting a good. *Blessings* upon food, people, or places are intentional acts of imbuing positive energy. *Creative visualization* and *mental rehearsal* techniques, used by athletes to improve performance, by patients to aid healing, and by people pursuing personal goals, are based on the principle of creating a clear, emotionally charged mental image of the desired outcome, as a way to attract or facilitate it. The simple act of *setting a clear intention* for the day, a meeting, or a project can help direct our focus, energy, and actions more effectively.

An ancient spiritual adage states, "energy follows thought." This encapsulates the idea that our thoughts are not passive, isolated mental events, but forms of energy and information with an inherent tendency to manifest in the world. The quality of our thoughts and, more importantly, the strength and clarity of our focused intentions, would determine the quality of the energy we emit and, consequently, the experiences we attract or create. Intention, when charged with positive emotion (like faith, love, gratitude) and held consistently, would be a powerful creative force in the participatory universe.

Recognizing the potential power of our intentions invites us to become more conscious and responsible for our inner world. Our thoughts and wills are not trivial; they carry energy and information that can reverberate through the fabric of reality. Cultivating positive thoughts, clarifying our intentions by aligning them with our deepest values, and focusing our mental energy with purpose and feeling may be the first steps towards shaping our life experience more consciously and constructively. The power of intention is not about magical, selfish control of the world, but about harmoniously participating in the creative dance between consciousness and the universe, a fundamental aspect of living the Quantum Soul.

Chapter 23
Manifestation

If our focused intention can exert a subtle influence on physical and biological systems, as suggested by psychokinesis research and the undeniable placebo effect, this leads us to an even broader and more personal application of this power: *manifestation*. This term, prominent in many contemporary spiritual currents and self-help literature, refers to the process of consciously bringing our desires, visions, or goals into physical reality, utilizing the creative power of our own consciousness in partnership with the universe. Far from being mere fantasy or superficial positive thinking, manifestation, when understood in a context integrating quantum, psychological, and spiritual insights, can be seen as a practical and empowering application of our nature as co-creators in a participatory universe.

What, then, does it mean to "manifest"? In essence, it is the process of making real, tangible, something that initially exists only as a thought, a mental image, a desire, or an intention. It is the art and science of translating an inner blueprint into an outer experience.

According to many metaphysical teachings, including those popularized under the label of the "Law of Attraction" (as in the work "The Secret"), the universe operates on a fundamental principle: like attracts like. Our predominant thoughts and emotions are not isolated, private events; they emit a vibrational signature, a specific energetic frequency. The universe, being itself a vast field of energy and potentiality, responds to this vibration, attracting into our experience circumstances, people, opportunities, and outcomes that resonate with our dominant frequency. Thoughts and feelings of joy, love, gratitude, and abundance would tend to attract corresponding positive experiences, while thoughts and feelings of fear, lack, anger, or resentment would tend to attract negative circumstances. The key to manifestation, in this view, would be to consciously align our inner vibration with what we wish to experience externally.

This idea of vibrations and attraction finds interesting metaphorical parallels in the quantum concepts we've explored. If the universe, at its fundamental level, is a field of potentialities (described by the wave function) waiting to be actualized by observation or interaction, then holding a clear, focused, and emotionally charged vision of the desired outcome could be analogous to repeatedly "collapsing" the wave function of our life in that specific direction. Our focused consciousness would act as the "observer" consistently selecting and actualizing that possibility among the many existing in the quantum field of our personal reality. We could also think of our mind as a "vibrational magnet." Our thoughts and emotions create a vibrational field around us, and this field interacts with the universal field of energy and information, attracting by resonance the experiences and opportunities matching our emission. Quantum physics, by revealing an interconnected, participatory, and probability-based universe, provides a conceptual backdrop where the idea that consciousness can influence reality becomes less implausible.

Concurrently, psychology offers well-established mechanisms supporting the effectiveness of mindset in achieving goals. The phenomenon of the *self-fulfilling prophecy* demonstrates that our beliefs and expectations about the future can indeed influence our behavior in ways (often unconscious) that help make those beliefs reality. If we deeply believe we will fail at a task, we might feel anxious, procrastinate, or not try hard enough, thus increasing the likelihood of failure. Conversely, if we believe in our ability to succeed, we tend to be more persistent, creative in problem-solving, and open to opportunities, which increases the chances of success. Studies on the "Pygmalion Effect" show how teachers' positive expectations can lead to better student performance, and how managers' expectations can influence employee productivity. Our mindset – whether optimistic or pessimistic, growth-oriented or fixed – creates filters through which we perceive the world and guides our actions, significantly shaping the outcomes we achieve.

Integrating these perspectives – the metaphysics of the Law of Attraction, quantum analogies, and psychological insights – we can see manifestation not as an instant magic trick or mere positive thinking detached from action, but as a dynamic process of *co-creation*. It's a partnership between our consciousness and the universe, involving both inner alignment and inspired action in the outer world. It's not enough to just wish for something; one must align thoughts, beliefs, and crucially, emotions with the desired reality, cultivating the feeling of already possessing it or of its inevitability. But one must also be attentive and act upon the ideas, intuitions, synchronicities, and opportunities the universe presents in response to our vibration and intention. Effective manifestation involves this harmonious dance between being (inner state) and doing (outer action).

Numerous examples, both anecdotal and in some research areas, illustrate this process. Elite athletes routinely use visualization and mental rehearsal techniques to program their bodies and minds for success, vividly imagining the perfect performance and feeling the emotion of victory even before competition. In healthcare, beyond the placebo effect, there are reports of patients using focused visualizations (like imagining defense cells fighting disease) as a complement to medical treatment, attributing part of their recovery or well-being to this mental practice. Many people attribute achieving significant goals in careers, relationships, or finances to consistently applying manifestation principles, such as setting clear intentions, practicing positive affirmations, cultivating gratitude, and acting confidently towards their dreams.

Several techniques can aid this inner alignment process for manifestation:

Creative Visualization: Creating vivid, detailed mental images of the desired outcome as if it were already real, involving all senses and, importantly, feeling the positive emotions associated with that reality (joy, gratitude, relief, love).

Positive Affirmations: Formulating and repeating short, positive, present-tense statements describing the desired reality as already existing (e.g., "I am healthy, prosperous, and happy," "Wonderful opportunities flow easily to me"). Repetition helps reprogram limiting subconscious beliefs.

Gratitude Practice: Deliberately cultivating feelings of appreciation for what one already has in life and also for the fulfillment of the desire as if it has already occurred. Gratitude is believed to raise vibrational frequency and open the flow to more abundance.

Acting "As If": Starting to make decisions and behave in ways aligned with the person you would be or the life you would have if your desire were already reality. This helps embody the new identity and signal your readiness to the universe.

It's important to approach manifestation with responsibility and ethical awareness. The goal should not be to control others or seek purely selfish gains at others' expense, but to create a reality aligned with our higher purpose and contributing to the general well-being. Intention should come from a place of integrity and love.

In sum, manifestation can be understood as a practical and empowering application of the principles of a conscious, interconnected, and participatory universe. It reminds us of our role as co-creators of our life experience. By learning to master our inner world – our thoughts, beliefs, and emotions – and aligning our actions with our highest intentions, we can begin to participate more consciously in the dance of creation, shaping our reality in partnership with the subtle laws of the cosmos. Conscious manifestation is an expression of the Quantum Soul in action, utilizing the power of the mind to weave the tapestry of its own journey.

Chapter 24
Quantum Healing

If we are fundamentally energetic beings, whose consciousness participates in creating reality and whose mind and body are intrinsically linked, how does this understanding transform our view of health, illness, and healing? Conventional medicine has made extraordinary progress by focusing on the physical and biochemical aspects of the body, often treating it like a complex machine fixable through external interventions like drugs and surgeries. However, a perspective integrating insights from quantum physics and spiritual wisdom suggests health is much more than the absence of physical disease. It involves a dynamic balance between body, mind, emotions, and spirit, and deep healing can be catalyzed by changes occurring at the subtlest levels of our consciousness and energy. It is in this context that the concept of "Quantum Healing" arises.

The term, popularized by authors like physician and writer Deepak Chopra, doesn't necessarily mean directly applying complex quantum equations to treat diseases. Instead, it points to a holistic approach to healing, recognizing the fundamental role of consciousness and energy in the health process. "Quantum Healing," in this broad sense, suggests significant health changes can occur when we access and influence the deeper levels of our physiology – levels where mind and matter meet, where energy and information organize biology. It invites us to go beyond treating symptoms to address the roots of illness, which may lie in energetic imbalances, chronic stress, emotional trauma, limiting beliefs, or spiritual disconnection.

The most robust scientific proof that the mind can directly influence the body's matter is, as mentioned, the *placebo effect*. It's a phenomenon so real and powerful it must be controlled for in all rigorous clinical trials evaluating new treatments. When a patient believes they are receiving an effective treatment (even if it's an inert substance), this belief can trigger a cascade of real physiological responses mimicking the active treatment's effects. The brain releases pain-relieving endorphins, the immune system can be activated or modulated, blood pressure might decrease, stress hormone levels can drop. In some conditions, the placebo response rate can reach 30%, 50%, or even higher, demonstrating the mind, through belief and expectation, acts as a powerful internal pharmacy, capable of producing tangible physical cures. The placebo effect isn't "imagination"; it's the mind healing the body.

In rarer, more dramatic cases, we witness the phenomenon of *spontaneous remission* – the unexpected, inexplicable recovery from serious diseases, like advanced cancer, without sufficient medical intervention to justify the cure. Although medical science often catalogs these events as statistical anomalies or incorrect diagnoses, research investigating common factors among people experiencing spontaneous remissions (like that conducted by the Institute of Noetic Sciences - IONS) often points to radical changes occurring in the individual's life and consciousness. These changes might include drastic shifts in diet and lifestyle, releasing deep repressed emotions (like anger or resentment, through forgiveness), finding a new sense of life purpose, cultivating positive emotions like love and joy, or developing intense, unwavering spiritual faith. While not proving direct causation, these cases suggest profound transformations in mind and spirit can, under certain circumstances, activate extremely potent self-healing mechanisms in the body, leading to recoveries seeming "miraculous" from a purely biomedical perspective.

Beyond the direct influence of the patient's own mind, many cultures and traditions have developed therapeutic practices aimed at working with the body's "subtle energy" to promote healing. These modalities, often labeled "energy healing" or, in popular jargon, "quantum healing," operate on the premise that a vital energy field (Chi, Prana, life force) animates the physical body and that illness arises from blockages or imbalances in this field. Examples include *Reiki* (a Japanese practice of channeling universal life energy through laying on of hands), *Pranic Healing* (working with cleansing and energizing the aura and chakras), *Johrei, spiritist passes* (transmitting spiritual fluids),

Therapeutic Touch, *acupuncture* (aiming to balance Chi flow through meridians using fine needles), and *homeopathy* (using extremely diluted substances, believed to carry an "energetic imprint" of the original substance capable of stimulating the body's life force).

Conventional science generally expresses skepticism towards these therapies, mainly because the "subtle energy fields" they claim to manipulate are not easily detectable or measurable by current scientific instruments, and because many rigorous studies have failed to consistently demonstrate their efficacy beyond the placebo effect. However, some research suggests potential benefits for certain conditions, like reducing pain, anxiety, or fatigue. From a "Quantum Healing" perspective, we might speculate these practices perhaps work by reorganizing energy or information patterns at a fundamental level. Perhaps the therapist's focused intention, or the channeled energy itself, interacts with quantum processes occurring in the patient's body molecules and cells (like neurotransmitter binding, enzyme activity, or gene expression), restoring coherence and harmony. Perhaps they work by resonance, where the therapist's or homeopathic remedy's coherent energy field helps restore coherence in the patient's field. Or perhaps they involve non-local effects, especially in cases of distance healing. Again, these are speculative interpretations seeking language for phenomena we don't fully understand, but pointing towards the possibility of healing occurring through manipulating energy and information at subtle levels.

The central point emerging from all these perspectives – placebo, spontaneous remissions, energy healing, and quantum speculations – is the confirmation of the profound unity among mind, body, emotions, and energy. Health isn't just a physical state; it's a state of holistic balance and harmony. Illness might manifest physically, but its roots can lie at subtler levels. Research in psychoneuroimmunology, for example, clearly demonstrates how chronic stress, negative emotions, and social isolation can suppress the immune system and increase disease susceptibility, while positive emotions, social connection, and relaxation practices can have protective effects.

True healing, therefore, involves addressing the human being in totality. This leads us to an *integrative* approach to health, where we combine the best of conventional medicine with practices nurturing mind, emotions, and spirit. *Meditation* and *mindfulness* are powerful examples, with proven benefits in stress reduction, decreasing inflammation, improving immune function, and even promoting neuroplasticity (the brain's ability to reorganize). *Creative visualization* can be used as a complementary tool to focus the mind on healing, imagine the body recovering, and strengthen the intention to get well. *Emotional healing* work, like therapy, trauma release, or forgiveness practice, can remove energetic and psychological blocks contributing to physical illness. Cultivating *positive intentions* for health, practicing gratitude, and nurturing faith and spiritual connection can also play important roles. And, of course, a healthy lifestyle – balanced diet, physical exercise, adequate sleep – provides the physical foundation for these subtle processes to operate effectively.

The Quantum Healing perspective offers us a hopeful and empowering view. It reminds us we are not passive victims of our biology, but active participants in our own health and well-being. By uniting scientific knowledge with inner wisdom and practices cultivating mind-body-spirit harmony, we can awaken our innate self-healing potential and move towards a deeper, more energetic, and conscious understanding of what it means to be truly healthy. It's about recognizing and honoring the Quantum Soul we are, an entity of consciousness and energy with the intrinsic capacity to seek balance and wholeness.

Chapter 25
Expansion of Consciousness

Our journey through the Quantum Soul has revealed a potentially vast being, interconnected with the cosmos in ways transcending space, time, and perhaps even familiar dimensions. We've seen how our consciousness might influence reality and how it could persist beyond the physical body. But these are not just theoretical ideas or distant potentials; the possibility of directly experiencing broader levels of reality, of expanding our consciousness beyond the limits of the everyday self, is a central promise of both spiritual traditions and some areas of contemporary psychology and research. Methods, practices, and experiences exist that can open us to states where perception deepens, boundaries dissolve, and we glimpse the more fundamental nature of ourselves and the universe.

Our ordinary consciousness, most of the time, operates in a mode focused on survival, navigating the physical world, managing our social identities and egoic concerns. We are often immersed in a stream of linear thoughts, processing sensory information, reacting to external and internal stimuli. While essential for daily life, this state of consciousness can be limited, filtering out much of the broader, subtler reality surrounding us and that we are.

Expanded states of consciousness, on the other hand, are characterized by a fundamental shift in this habitual perception. In them, the sense of a separate self may diminish or disappear, giving way to feelings of unity with others, nature, or the entire cosmos. Time might seem to stop or become irrelevant. A profound sense of peace, love, or joy can emerge, along with intuitive insights or direct understandings about the nature of reality that transcend ordinary logic.

Throughout history, various cultures developed contemplative practices aimed at inducing or facilitating these expanded states. *Meditation*, in its many forms (like mindfulness meditation, cultivating present moment awareness; concentration meditation, focusing the mind on a single object; or transcendental meditation, using mantras), aims to quiet the mind's incessant chatter, disidentify consciousness from the flow of thoughts and emotions, and open an inner space for direct perception of deeper levels of being. States of deep meditative absorption, known as *samadhi* (in Yoga) or *satori* (in Zen Buddhism), are described as experiences of enlightenment or union with ultimate reality.

Yoga, far beyond physical postures (*asanas*), is a holistic system integrating conscious breathing (*pranayama*), concentration (*dharana*), meditation (*dhyana*), and ethical principles, all aimed at purifying body and mind, balancing subtle energies, and preparing the way for consciousness expansion. Specific *breathing* techniques, like Holotropic Breathwork developed by psychiatrist Stanislav Grof, or other forms of connected, accelerated breathing, are also used to induce altered states of consciousness, allowing access to deep memories, repressed emotions, and sometimes transpersonal or mystical experiences.

Within religious traditions, *contemplative prayer* and mystical practices seek a direct, experiential union with the Divine, often through silence, surrender, and openness to the sacred presence.

Although the subjective nature of these experiences makes them difficult to study objectively, modern neuroscience has begun mapping some brain correlates associated with these states and practices. Studies with experienced meditators using electroencephalography (EEG) have shown distinct brainwave patterns during deep meditation, such as increased alpha and theta waves (associated with relaxation, inner focus, and hypnagogic states) and, in some cases of compassion or ecstatic meditation, the presence of high-amplitude, synchronized gamma waves across vast brain areas. This high gamma synchrony is interpreted by some researchers as a possible neural correlate of states of unified consciousness, high mental clarity, and information integration. Furthermore, research on *neuroplasticity* demonstrates that regular meditation practice can lead to lasting structural and functional changes in the brain, strengthening areas related to attention, emotional regulation, empathy, and self-awareness. Science is beginning to validate the benefits and depth of transformations induced by these ancient practices.

The culminating experiences of these practices, often called *mystical* or peak experiences, share remarkably similar characteristics, regardless of the cultural or religious context. Philosopher and psychologist William James, in his classic study "The Varieties of Religious Experience," identified four main marks: *ineffability* (the experience defies description in words), *noetic quality* (it brings a sense of deep insight, direct, true knowledge), *transiency* (they are usually short-lived states), and *passivity* (the feeling of being grasped or guided by a higher force). Additionally, these experiences often involve an overwhelming sense of *unity* or fusion with the whole, *transcendence* of normal categories of space and time, a profound sense of *sacredness* or numinosity, and intensely positive emotions like peace, joy, unconditional love, and reverence.

Interestingly, in some cultures, psychoactive substances derived from plants (sometimes called "power plants" or *entheogens*, meaning "generating the divine within") have been and are used in ritual and sacred contexts as tools to induce expanded states of consciousness. Ayahuasca in the Amazon, peyote among some Native North American tribes, or psilocybin mushrooms in certain Mesoamerican traditions, were historically used by shamans and healers not for recreational purposes, but to facilitate healing, divination, connection with the spirit world, and gaining knowledge. In these induced states, practitioners often report journeys to other realities, encounters with archetypal or spiritual entities, and profound insights about themselves and the cosmos, experiences echoing descriptions of spontaneous mystical experiences and those achieved through contemplative practices. The recent rediscovery of these substances' therapeutic potential by Western science (e.g., research with psilocybin for depression, end-of-life anxiety, and addiction) has also highlighted their capacity to induce mystical-type experiences that seem to correlate with lasting psychological benefits. This suggests different paths – contemplative or chemical (used with respect and appropriate intention) – can sometimes lead to similar states of consciousness expansion.

How can we understand these states from the perspective of the Quantum Soul? Perhaps we can use the metaphor of consciousness as a radio or tuner. In our normal state, we are tuned to the frequency of everyday physical reality. Consciousness expansion practices could be seen as methods to adjust this radio's "dial," allowing us to tune into other frequencies, other channels of information and experience normally beyond our reach. Perhaps in these states, our consciousness manages to interact more directly with the Unified Field, the Collective Unconscious, or the Akashic Field, accessing normally veiled information and levels of reality. Perhaps the brain, in these moments, achieves a state of greater coherence (possibly even macroscopic quantum coherence, as speculated by some), enabling radically different modes of perception and processing.

It's important to remember that consciousness expansion needn't be a dramatic or rare event reserved for mystics or entheogen users. We can cultivate greater breadth of awareness in daily life through simple practices. *Mindfulness*, practicing intentional, non-judgmental attention to the present moment, helps us step out of mental autopilot and perceive more directly the richness of sensory experience, the impermanent nature of thoughts, and the subtle interconnection between ourselves and the environment. Cultivating moments of *awe and wonder* at the beauty of nature, art, or an act of kindness can momentarily lift us out of egoic concerns and connect us to something larger. Actively practicing *compassion* and *universal love*, extending well wishes to all beings, expands our circle of identification beyond ourselves. Engaging in creative activities or others leading to *flow states*, where we feel fully immersed and lose track of time and the separate self, can also be a form of expansion.

Ultimately, the quest for consciousness expansion isn't just about having extraordinary experiences, but about fostering deep, lasting personal growth. People integrating these experiences often report increased empathy and compassion, decreased fear of death, greater clarity about life purpose, enhanced creativity, and a greater capacity for love and service. These are the fruits of inner evolution, recognized by both transpersonal psychology (studying the highest potentials of human nature) and spiritual traditions aiming for enlightenment or self-realization. Expanding our consciousness is perhaps the most fundamental task in our journey to understand and fully embody our nature as Quantum Souls, beings of light and unlimited potential participating in the cosmic dance of creation.

Chapter 26
Synchronicity

Our exploration of hidden connections in nature, like non-locality and entanglement, showed us the universe might be interconnected in ways challenging our linear understanding of cause and effect. Now, let's turn to a different kind of mysterious connection, one seemingly operating not through direct physical influences, but through *meaning* and *pattern*: synchronicity. Coined by Swiss psychologist Carl Gustav Jung, the term describes those "meaningful coincidences" that surprise and delight us, events seemingly connected so relevantly they defy explanation by mere chance, suggesting a hidden order or underlying intelligence operating in our lives.

We've all experienced moments like these, leaving us with a sense of awe or that something deeper is happening. You think intensely about a friend you haven't spoken to in years, and moments later, the phone rings – it's them. You're struggling with a specific question, and upon randomly opening a book or overhearing a stranger's conversation, you find the exact answer needed. You have a vivid dream featuring a rare, obscure symbol, and the next day, you encounter that same symbol repeatedly in unexpected places. Or perhaps a series of apparently unrelated events – a chance meeting, unexpected information, an opportunity arising out of nowhere – converges almost miraculously to solve a complex problem or open a new path in your life. These occurrences, when charged with a strong sense of personal meaning and perfect timing, are classic examples of synchronicity. They are distinguished from mere statistical coincidences (like two people in the same room sharing a birthday) by their numinous quality, the feeling there's a message or purpose behind the coincidence.

It was Carl Jung who first systematically investigated this phenomenon and named it. He defined synchronicity as an *acausal connecting principle*. Unlike causality, describing the familiar link between cause and effect through time, synchronicity would describe the connection between events (usually an inner psychic event, like a thought or dream, and an outer physical event) occurring roughly simultaneously (or in close temporal succession) whose connection lies in their shared *meaning* or symbolic pattern, not in a direct influence of one upon the other.

For Jung, these meaningful coincidences were not mere chance but manifestations of an underlying order in nature, a pre-established harmony or a dynamic connecting the individual psyche to the material world through meaning. He believed synchronicity was particularly likely to occur during moments of high emotional charge, personal transformation, or when powerful archetypes from the collective unconscious were activated in the individual's psyche.

Jung speculated the *Collective Unconscious*, with its universal archetypes, might play a mediating role in synchronicity occurrences. When an individual is deeply engaged with an archetype (whether through dreams, therapeutic work, or life challenges), this archetypal energy could somehow "organize" or "attract" events in the outer world symbolically mirroring the inner process. It would be as if psyche and matter were two aspects of the same underlying reality, capable of resonating and reflecting each other through shared meaning.

Fascinatingly, Jung developed his ideas on synchronicity in collaboration and dialogue with physicist Wolfgang Pauli, a quantum mechanics pioneer and Nobel laureate. Pauli, initially skeptical, became deeply interested in the concept, recognizing parallels between synchronicity's acausal nature and certain aspects of quantum physics, like non-local correlations in entanglement (where distant particles' states are linked without a local cause traveling between them). Although they didn't reach a complete theory, Jung and Pauli speculated together that synchronicity might represent a fundamental principle of nature, complementary to causality, perhaps emerging from the interaction between physics laws and psyche dynamics. Pauli even suggested future science would need to incorporate both physics and depth psychology to fully understand reality.

While quantum physics doesn't provide a direct explanation for synchronicity in the Jungian sense (involving meaning and consciousness), we can draw some conceptual analogies. Just as entanglement reveals acausal correlations between distant physical systems, synchronicity suggests acausal correlations between mental states and physical events, based on meaning. Could individual consciousness, by focusing on certain themes or archetypes, subtly influence the quantum probability field of the environment, making the manifestation of events resonating meaningfully with the inner state more likely? This is a speculation leading back to the idea of a participatory universe, where consciousness isn't separate from the world but interacts with it in ways beyond classical causality.

In the spiritual and personal development sphere, synchronicities are often interpreted very directly and practically: as *messages* or *signs* from the Universe, God, spirit guides, or our own Higher Self. They can be seen as confirmations we're on the right path, answers to questions we've asked, alerts to pay attention to something important, or divine "nudges" guiding us in a specific direction. Experiencing an increasing flow of synchronicities is often considered a sign we are living in greater alignment with our soul purpose and the cosmos's greater intelligence. This perspective invites a symbolic reading of life events, seeking hidden meaning behind coincidences, and trusting the subtle guidance the universe seems to offer.

It's important, of course, to approach interpreting synchronicities with balance and discernment. The human tendency to find patterns and meaning can sometimes lead us to see connections where none exist or over-interpret trivial coincidences. Avoiding superstition and maintaining critical thinking is necessary. However, denying the possibility of genuinely meaningful coincidences would be closing our eyes to a mysterious and potentially important aspect of human experience. The invitation is to cultivate *mindfulness* of our life events, notice coincidences that touch us deeply, reflect on their possible *personal* meaning (as meaning is often subjective), and use these occurrences as opportunities for introspection and growth, without necessarily building grandiose theories about them. Keeping a synchronicity journal can be a useful tool for observing patterns and deepening understanding.

Ultimately, the phenomenon of synchronicity reinforces the view of a universe where mind and matter, inner and outer, are not rigidly separated but in constant, mysterious dialogue. It suggests reality might have a dimension of meaning and pattern operating parallel to physical causality laws. The occurrence of meaningful coincidences points to a deeper connection, perhaps mediated by information fields or collective consciousness itself, where our inner states can mirror or manifest in outer events in subtle yet powerful ways. Synchronicity reminds us we live in a potentially intelligent and responsive cosmos, a universe that not only exists but perhaps also speaks to us through the language of symbols and meaning, reinforcing the profound unity between the Quantum Soul and the tapestry of existence.

Chapter 27
Ancient Wisdom

As we navigate the deep and sometimes turbulent waters of quantum physics and its implications for consciousness and reality, the impression might arise that we are dealing with entirely new ideas, revolutionary concepts radically breaking from the entire history of human thought. However, turning our gaze to the great traditions of spiritual and philosophical wisdom that flourished in different cultures and eras, we discover something remarkable: many insights now seemingly emerging from the forefront of science find surprising, sometimes almost literal, parallels in the teachings of sages, mystics, and philosophers who lived centuries or even millennia ago. It seems human intuition, through deep introspection, subtle observation of nature, and direct mystical experience, was able to glimpse fundamental truths about the cosmos that modern science is only beginning to rediscover and validate with its own language and methodology. This convergence between ancient and modern knowledge not only validates both approaches but also offers us a richer, more integrated understanding of reality and our place within it.

At the heart of India's philosophical and religious traditions, particularly in *Vedanta* (the culmination of the Vedas), we find concepts resonating powerfully with the quantum and holistic view. The notion of *Brahman* describes the Ultimate Reality, the one, immanent and transcendent, undifferentiated, unchanging Cosmic Consciousness, the source and substance of all existence. Everything we see and experience would merely be a manifestation or appearance (*Maya*) of this single reality. Concurrently, *Atman* represents the individual soul, the deepest Self of each being, which, in essence, is identical to Brahman. The famous Vedic maxim *"Tat Tvam Asi"* ("Thou Art That") expresses this fundamental unity between the individual and the absolute. How can we not see here a parallel with the scientific search for a Unified Field, the idea of an underlying universal Consciousness (as in quantum idealism or panpsychism), and the quantum perception of matter as an energetic and perhaps illusory manifestation in its apparent solidity (echoing *Maya*)?

Buddhism, emerging from the Hindu context, deepens the analysis of reality's nature with the concepts of *Shunyata* (Emptiness) and *Pratītyasamutpāda* (Dependent Origination). Shunyata doesn't mean nihilism or that nothing exists, but that all phenomena, including ourselves, are "empty" of inherent, independent, permanent existence. Nothing possesses an isolated essence; everything arises and exists dependent on causes and conditions, in a vast web of interconnection. Dependent Origination precisely describes this web of mutual relationships, where everything affects and is affected by everything else. This view of a fluid, interconnected reality devoid of autonomous entities finds striking resonance with the quantum picture of the universe, where particles are non-locally entangled, where reality emerges from relationships and interactions, and where impermanence (*Anicca*, another central Buddhist concept) is reflected in the constant flow of energy and information in quantum fields.

In ancient China's *Taoism*, we find the concept of the *Tao*, the "Way," the primordial source and ineffable ordering principle permeating all nature, operating spontaneously and effortlessly (*Wu Wei*). The Tao manifests through the dynamic interaction of two polar, complementary forces, *Yin* (feminine, passive, dark, receptive) and *Yang* (masculine, active, light, penetrating). The harmonious balance between Yin and Yang is seen as key to health and harmony in the individual and the cosmos. Again, we can draw parallels: the Tao as analogous to a Unified Field or Bohm's implicate order; and the dynamic complementarity of Yin and Yang echoing Bohr's Principle of Complementarity (wave/particle) and other fundamental dualities (energy/matter, positive/negative) resolving into a greater unity in physics.

Returning to the West, esoteric and philosophical traditions also offer glimpses of this converging wisdom. *Hermeticism*, a tradition dating back to ancient Egypt and Hellenistic Greece, encapsulated in texts like the *Kybalion*, enunciates principles seemingly prefiguring modern discoveries. The Principle of

Mentalism ("THE ALL is MIND; The Universe is Mental") aligns with idealist or participatory views of reality where consciousness is primary. The Principle of Correspondence ("As above, so below; as below, so above") echoes the idea of a holographic or fractal universe, with patterns repeating at different scales (microcosm/macrocosm). The Principle of Vibration ("Nothing rests; everything moves; everything vibrates") anticipates the modern view of matter as constantly vibrating energy.

In classical Greek philosophy, Plato spoke of a transcendental realm of perfect *Forms* or Ideas, of which the physical world was merely an imperfect shadow – an idea speculatively relatable to modern concepts of information fields or archetypes shaping manifest reality. Heraclitus, with his famous maxim *"Panta rhei"* ("Everything flows"), captured the dynamic, impermanent nature of reality that modern physics would later confirm.

Indigenous and *shamanic traditions* worldwide, though diverse, often share an animistic worldview where spirit or life force permeates all nature – rivers, mountains, plants, animals. They emphasize the deep interconnection of all life and the existence of non-ordinary realities or dimensions accessible through altered states of consciousness, knowledge resonating with the holism, potential panpsychism, and multidimensionality we've discussed.

Even in more recent traditions, like *Spiritism* codified by Allan Kardec in the 19th century, we find concepts dialoguing with the emerging view. The central notion of the *perispirit* – a semi-material, fluidic body serving as the link between the immortal soul and the physical body, persisting after death and evolving through multiple incarnations – can be seen as an intuitive description of a bioenergetic field or subtle body, perhaps related to quantum fields associated with consciousness or the quantum information some theorize might survive brain death. Spiritism's emphasis on the spirit's moral and intellectual evolution through successive experiences also aligns with the broader theme of consciousness development and expansion permeating our investigation.

What emerges from this brief overview is a striking vision of convergence between ancient and modern knowledge. Sages and mystics from different cultures, using introspection, contemplation, and direct experience as their investigative tools, seem to have accessed profound insights into the fundamental nature of reality – its underlying unity, its energetic and vibrational nature, its impermanence, the relativity of perception, the creative power of the mind, and the existence of dimensions or levels of being beyond the physical. These truths, expressed through symbolic, mythical, and philosophical languages, are being, in a way, rediscovered and corroborated by modern science, which reaches similar conclusions through its own rigorous methodology of external observation, experimentation, and mathematical modeling.

This doesn't mean science is simply "proving" spirituality, or that ancient views were identical to current scientific theories in every detail. It does mean we can recognize science and spirituality as potentially converging paths in the human quest for truth and understanding. The "novelty" of quantum discoveries often lies in confirming, in a new language, the "antiquity" of spiritual wisdom.

This perception invites us to cultivate deep respect for ancestral knowledge and recognize that intuition and inner experience can be valid sources of knowledge about reality, complementary to scientific investigation. Integrating these two great ways of knowing offers us a much richer and more complete foundation for understanding the universe and our place in it, recognizing the Quantum Soul as an entity whose nature resonates across ages and cultures, from the atom to the absolute.

Chapter 28
Current Convergence

After centuries of a separation often seen as insurmountable, where science focused on the objective material world and spirituality on the inner realm of faith and subjective experience, we are today, on April 4th, 2025, witnessing a fascinating and growing movement towards dialogue, integration, and convergence. The revolutionary ideas of quantum physics, the persistent mysteries of consciousness, neuroscience discoveries about brain plasticity and meditation's effects, coupled with a rediscovery and revaluation of ancestral wisdom, are creating fertile ground for the ancient walls between science and spirit to begin crumbling. We live in a historical moment of potential synthesis, where a more holistic and integrated worldview seems to be emerging.

This rapprochement is not just theoretical; it manifests in concrete initiatives and the work of individuals and institutions dedicated to building bridges. A notable example is the *Mind and Life Institute*, co-founded by neuroscientist Francisco Varela, entrepreneur Adam Engle, and His Holiness the Dalai Lama. Since 1987, the institute has promoted rigorous, collaborative dialogues between the Dalai Lama and world-renowned scientists – physicists, neuroscientists, psychologists, biologists – exploring crucial themes like the nature of consciousness, perception, destructive emotions, compassion, and ethics. These pioneering conversations not only generated mutual respect between Buddhist contemplative traditions and modern science but also inspired new lines of scientific research on meditation's effects and the human mind's potential.

Another key organization in this landscape is the *Institute of Noetic Sciences (IONS)*, founded in 1973 by Apollo 14 astronaut Dr. Edgar Mitchell. After his transformative experience in space, where he had a direct perception of the cosmos's unity and interconnectedness (the "Overview Effect"), Mitchell dedicated his life to promoting rigorous scientific investigation of "noetic sciences" – the study of consciousness's potential and powers. IONS has sponsored and conducted research on phenomena like meditation, distance healing, extrasensory perception, near-death experiences, and the very nature of consciousness, seeking to apply scientific methods to explore aspects of reality transcending the materialistic paradigm.

Besides these institutions, we see a growing number of respected scientists in their fields who, without abandoning scientific rigor, show openness to exploring traditionally spiritual or metaphysical topics. Physicist Fritjof Capra, as early as 1975 with his bestseller "The Tao of Physics," drew eloquent parallels between modern physics concepts (quantum and relativity) and Eastern mysticism teachings. Physicist

Amit Goswami has become a prominent advocate for quantum idealism, arguing consciousness is the foundation of reality. Biologists like Rupert Sheldrake, though controversial, challenge materialistic dogmas with theories on morphic fields. Neuroscientists like Richard Davidson at the University of Wisconsin-Madison conduct cutting-edge research on the neural bases of meditation and positive emotions, often collaborating with experienced contemplatives. Medical researchers like Pim van Lommel and Bruce Greyson publish studies on near-death experiences in peer-reviewed medical journals, bringing the topic into serious scientific debate. Psychologists like Stanislav Grof helped found transpersonal psychology, a branch explicitly studying the spiritual and transcendent dimensions of human experience. These voices, coming from within the scientific community itself, are crucial for legitimizing and expanding the dialogue.

Parallel to these academic and research developments, we observe the remarkable integration of practices once considered esoteric or exclusively spiritual into mainstream culture. *Mindfulness meditation*, derived from Buddhist practices but often presented secularly, has exploded in popularity over recent decades. It's now taught in hospitals, schools, corporations, and psychotherapy centers, with a vast scientific literature documenting its benefits for stress reduction, anxiety, depression, improved attention, emotional regulation, and general well-being. Neuroscience has validated what contemplatives knew for centuries: training the mind through meditation can actually change the brain and improve quality of life.

Similarly, *integrative medicine* is gaining increasing ground, seeking to combine effective conventional medical treatments with complementary approaches treating the whole person – mind, body, and spirit. Therapies like acupuncture, yoga, tai chi, reiki, therapeutic massage, and nutritional and lifestyle counseling are increasingly offered in hospitals and clinics as part of more holistic care.

This trend reflects a growing dissatisfaction with the limitations of a strictly materialistic worldview, which reduces reality solely to physical matter and energy and considers consciousness a mere byproduct of the brain. Within science itself, voices rise calling for a paradigm expansion. In 2014, a group of scientists published the "Manifesto for a Post-Materialist Science," arguing the materialist dogma imposes unnecessary restrictions on scientific inquiry and that it's time for science to seriously study mind and consciousness as fundamental aspects of reality, exploring phenomena like psi and consciousness survival with rigorous methods but without philosophical prejudice.

It's true this convergence also reflects, sometimes confusingly or superficially, in popular culture. Terms like "quantum" are often used vaguely in self-help or spiritual contexts ("quantum healing," "quantum leap," "quantum thinking"), frequently without real understanding of the underlying physics. However, even this somewhat imprecise popularization indicates a genuine collective fascination with the possibility of uniting modern science and spirituality, a deep desire for a worldview integrating objective knowledge with subjective experience and a sense of purpose.

Beyond the popular buzz, serious initiatives continue pushing frontiers. Increasingly sophisticated experiments investigate mind-matter interaction. Longitudinal studies track the effects of contemplative practices on the brain and health over time. Complex theoretical models attempt to describe the nature of consciousness and its relation to physics. Universities worldwide are starting to offer courses and even graduate programs focused on the intersection of science, consciousness, spirituality, and well-being.

We are, therefore, living in an era of remarkable *synthesis*. The old Cartesian divisions between mind and matter, subject and object, science and spirit, are becoming increasingly porous and questioned. We realize a complete understanding of reality likely requires integrating multiple forms of knowledge: rigorous investigation of the outer world through the scientific method, and disciplined exploration of the inner world through introspection, contemplation, and direct experience. It's not about choosing between reason and intuition, but honoring and integrating both.

This current convergence is more than a mere intellectual trend; it signals the potential birth of a new paradigm for the 21st century – a more holistic, integrated, and conscious paradigm. Living in this historical moment offers us the unique opportunity to actively participate in this synthesis, to build bridges between ancestral wisdom and modern knowledge, not just to expand our understanding of the universe and ourselves, but also to inspire more creative and compassionate solutions to the challenges we face as humanity. The convergence between science and spirituality isn't just about reconciling ideas; it's about catalyzing the next stage of conscious evolution on our planet.

Chapter 29
Practical Applications

Throughout this book, we've journeyed through the frontiers of modern physics and ancient wisdom, exploring a vision of reality where energy and consciousness are fundamental, where the universe is interconnected, participatory, and potentially multidimensional. We've grasped, conceptually, that we might be more than just isolated physical bodies; we are "Quantum Souls," beings of energy and consciousness with far greater potential than we imagined. But how does this profound understanding translate into our daily lives? How can we apply these insights to live more fully, consciously, and fulfilled? This chapter aims precisely to build that bridge, transforming abstract concepts into practical tools and concrete examples for everyday life. Knowledge of our quantum nature isn't just for intellectual contemplation; it's a call to a new way of being and acting in the world.

One of the most direct and powerful applications lies in the conscious use of our intention. If we live in a participatory universe where our observation and focus can influence probabilities, we can start each day with an intentional practice. Set aside a few moments in the morning, before diving into the day's hustle, to visualize or set a clear intention for the hours ahead. How do you wish your day to unfold? What qualities do you want to embody (peace, efficiency, joy, compassion)? What positive outcomes would you like to see? Utilize *creative visualization*: vividly imagine your day flowing harmoniously, see yourself handling challenges calmly and wisely, feel the satisfaction of your interactions and accomplishments. By doing this, you're not just preparing psychologically, but potentially "projecting" an energetic frequency, "collapsing" favorable probabilities in the quantum field of your day. It's an act of conscious co-creation of your immediate future.

Another crucial area is managing our inner state, our energetic "vibration." If our thoughts and emotions emit frequencies attracting corresponding experiences (as suggested by the Law of Attraction and the idea of resonance), cultivating self-awareness becomes fundamental. The practice of *mindfulness* is an essential tool here. Throughout the day, try observing your thoughts and emotions without judgment. Notice habitual patterns: do you tend to ruminate on worries? Criticize yourself or others? Focus on lack? These patterns generate low energy frequencies that can perpetuate negative cycles. Awareness is the first step towards change. Once aware, you can consciously choose to shift focus. Actively cultivate thoughts and feelings of *gratitude* for what you already have, *compassion* for yourself and others, *optimism* about the future, and *joy* in small moments. This doesn't mean ignoring difficulties, but choosing not to be dominated by negative vibrations. By raising your predominant inner frequency, you energetically align with more positive and harmonious experiences.

In interpersonal relationships, understanding unity and quantum entanglement can cultivate what we might call *quantum empathy*. When conflicts, disagreements, or hurt arise, remember: on a fundamental level, we are not separate. The person before you, even if their actions or words bother you, is part of the same cosmic web as you. Harming another, energetically or emotionally, ultimately harms yourself. This perception can soften judgment, facilitate communication from a place of understanding, and make forgiveness (of self and other) a more natural process. Try seeing beyond superficial behavior and connecting with the essence, the shared "Quantum Soul," existing beneath ego masks. This can radically transform the dynamic of your relationships.

In the workplace, studies, or creative projects, we can learn to integrate rational analysis with *intuition*. While logic and planning are important, the quantum view reminds us we also have access to a vast field of information and creative potential (be it the collective unconscious, morphic fields, or the quantum field itself). Be open to sudden insights, "gut feelings," ideas seemingly coming "out of nowhere." Trust these intuitive flashes as valuable messages. By combining rigorous analysis with receptivity to intuition, we can find more innovative solutions, make wiser decisions, and navigate challenges with greater fluidity and creativity.

In health, the Quantum Soul perspective encourages adopting a truly holistic approach, integrating care for the physical body, mind, emotions, and energy. Incorporate mind-body practices into your daily or weekly routine. Regular *meditation*, even for a few minutes daily, can drastically reduce stress levels (lowering cortisol and inflammation), clear the mind, and strengthen inner connection. *Conscious movement* practices like Yoga, Tai Chi, or Qigong help release tensions, harmonize vital energy flow (Chi/Prana), and integrate body and mind. *Conscious breathing* is a simple, powerful tool, always available, to calm the nervous system and center awareness in the present. View these practices not as chores, but as essential acts of self-care and maintenance for your physical-energetic vehicle.

We see examples of these applications in the world. Elite athletes visualizing victory with intensity and detail, programming their minds and bodies for peak performance. Successful entrepreneurs attributing part of their results to clear vision, unwavering positive mindset, and the ability to act on intuition. Companies implementing mindfulness programs to reduce employee stress, increase focus, and stimulate creativity. These examples make palpable the idea that our inner states and mental focus have real, measurable consequences in the outer world.

We can also extend this energetic awareness to our *environments*. Our homes, workplaces, and the spaces we frequent also possess a "vibration." We can positively influence it through simple actions like maintaining organization and cleanliness, bringing in natural elements (plants, natural light), using colors, sounds, or scents that uplift us, or even through the conscious intention to energetically "cleanse" or "bless" the space. Equally important is the energy of the people we associate with. Surrounding ourselves with positive, constructive, supportive people creates beneficial collective resonance (a positive egregore), while constant exposure to negativity can drain our energy. Consciously choosing our environments and company is also a form of energy management.

Finally, understanding an interconnected, responsive universe reminds us of the ancient spiritual principle of the *law of return* or *karma*: what we emit into the universe – in thoughts, words, emotions, and actions – tends to return to us somehow. Living with integrity, acting with kindness, thinking with compassion are not just moral precepts, but attitudes aligning us with the harmonious flow of a cosmos where everything is linked and everything reverberates.

In summary, perceiving oneself as a Quantum Soul isn't a purely philosophical exercise; it's an invitation to live differently. It offers a toolkit and perspectives for navigating life with more awareness, intention, creativity, and connection. By applying these principles – using focused intention, managing inner vibration, cultivating quantum empathy, integrating intuition, caring for holistic health, and creating resonant environments – we shift from passive spectators to active participants in co-creating our reality. It's the path to embodying, in daily practice, the profound truth of our energetic and conscious nature in a living, interconnected universe.

Chapter 30
Evolution of Consciousness

Our exploration of the Quantum Soul has revealed an image of the human being and the universe that is dynamic, interconnected, and profoundly participatory. We've seen that consciousness is not a mere passive spectator, but a fundamental, perhaps even primary, element in the tapestry of reality. If consciousness is so central, is it static and unchanging, or is it itself subject to a process of development, of evolution? The answer, echoing in both scientific theories about cognitive evolution and deep spiritual teachings about the soul's journey, seems to be a resounding yes. Consciousness, both at the individual level and the collective level of humanity, appears to be on a trajectory of continuous unfolding, and the current moment, with its unprecedented convergence of science and spirituality, may represent a particularly crucial stage in this evolution.

We can trace, in broad strokes, a possible trajectory of human consciousness evolution throughout history. In early times, human consciousness seemed more immersed in nature, guided by survival instincts, primal fears, and strong identification with the group or tribe (*archaic* or *instinctual* consciousness). With the development of language and symbolic thought, emerged a *magical* and *mythic* consciousness, where the world was explained through myths, rituals, and invisible forces, and participation in the cosmos was felt more directly, though less differentiated. Gradually, especially with the advent of agriculture, cities, writing, and Greek philosophy, *mental-rational* consciousness developed. Logic, abstract reason, analysis, and conceptual thought became powerful tools for understanding and manipulating the world. The individual emerged with stronger self-awareness, but often at the cost of a sense of separation from nature and the whole. The Scientific Revolution and the Enlightenment represented the peak of this rational phase, bringing immense technological advancements and a mechanistic understanding of the universe, but also deepening the divide between matter and spirit, subject and object.

Today, many philosophers, psychologists, and spiritual thinkers suggest we are potentially entering a new phase, a phase of *integrative* or *holistic* consciousness. Driven by globalization, the ecological crisis forcing us to recognize our planetary interdependence, ethical challenges of new technologies, and crucially, the convergence between cutting-edge science discoveries (like quantum physics) and the rediscovery of contemplative wisdom, we are called to transcend and include previous stages. Integrative consciousness seeks to harmonize reason with intuition, analytical thought with holistic perception, individual autonomy with collective responsibility, scientific understanding with spiritual experience. It recognizes the validity of multiple ways of knowing and seeks a worldview honoring both matter and spirit, brain and mind, part and whole.

This idea of progressive consciousness development finds strong support in the spiritual perspective viewing life as a *school for the soul*. Many traditions, especially those including belief in reincarnation, teach our existence isn't limited to one life but is part of a long evolutionary journey. Each incarnation, with its challenges, relationships, learnings, and service opportunities, would be a chance for the soul (or individual consciousness) to develop essential qualities like wisdom, love, compassion, humility, and self-awareness. Sufferings and difficulties wouldn't be punishments, but valuable lessons designed for our growth. In this view, life itself becomes a cosmic curriculum for consciousness expansion.

Some thinkers have tried applying this evolutionary perspective not just to individuals, but to humanity as a whole. The aforementioned Teilhard de Chardin, with his vision of the *Noosphere* and the *Omega Point*, postulated cosmic evolution has an inherent direction (orthogenesis) towards increasing complexity and interiorization of consciousness. He predicted a future where human consciousness, driven by socialization and technology, would unify on a planetary scale, culminating in a point of convergence and union with the Divine. Contemporary thinker Peter Russell also speaks of the possibility of an exponential acceleration in consciousness evolution, a kind of "consciousness explosion" analogous to the Cambrian explosion in biological evolution, perhaps driven by global crisis and the rapid spread of transformative information and practices.

Can we identify signs in the world today seemingly corroborating the idea that a significant shift in collective consciousness is underway? The growing concern for global humanitarian issues, human rights, social justice, and especially the ecological crisis, suggests an expansion of the circle of empathy beyond family, tribe, or nation, encompassing all humanity and even other life forms. The unprecedented interest in practices like meditation, mindfulness, yoga, psychotherapy, and various forms of non-dogmatic spirituality indicates a collective hunger for meaning, inner well-being, and self-knowledge beyond purely materialistic values. Information technology itself, with the internet connecting billions of minds in an instantaneous global network, can be seen as a physical infrastructure for the emerging Noosphere, accelerating idea exchange and the formation of planetary awareness – though it also presents risks of misinformation and polarization.

The Spiritist perspective, codified by Allan Kardec, offers a detailed framework for this evolution of consciousness in a cosmic context. It postulates that spirits (individual souls) continuously progress through multiple incarnations, not just on Earth, but on countless worlds of different evolutionary degrees in the universe – from primitive worlds, through worlds of trial and expiation (like Earth currently), worlds of regeneration, to blissful or celestial worlds. The goal of this journey is moral and intellectual perfection, ever approaching relative perfection and happiness. Earthly humanity itself, as a collectivity of spirits at a similar evolutionary stage, would be undergoing a transition period, moving towards becoming a "world of regeneration," where good will prevail over evil. This view offers an optimistic and teleological (goal-oriented) framework for human and cosmic history.

How does this grand narrative of consciousness evolution relate to our individual lives? It invites us to see our own struggles, learnings, and personal growth not as isolated, meaningless events, but as integral parts of this vast cosmic evolutionary process. Every step we take towards greater self-awareness, every act of compassion, every overcoming of a limiting pattern, every quest for wisdom and truth contributes not only to our own evolution but also to raising collective consciousness. By striving to become better versions of ourselves, we are, in fact, helping drive the evolution of humanity itself.

In this context, the "quantum-spiritual" worldview this book seeks to present should be seen not as an endpoint, but as a crucial catalyst for the current phase of consciousness evolution. By helping us recognize our energetic nature, fundamental interconnectedness, co-creative potential, and the primacy of consciousness, this integrated view provides the map and motivation to participate more consciously in this evolutionary journey. It encourages us to build bridges between scientific knowledge and heart wisdom, between personal development and service to the common good. The evolution of consciousness is the great adventure of our time, and each Quantum Soul is called to play its unique, irreplaceable role in this magnificent unfolding towards a future of greater light, love, and understanding.

Chapter 31
Cosmic Purpose

Having explored the energetic nature of reality, the mystery of consciousness, the dance between matter and spirit, the non-local connections uniting us, and the possibility of consciousness's continuous evolution, we inevitably arrive at the most fundamental human question: *Why?* Why does this vast, intricate universe exist? Why did life arise on a small blue planet? Why did consciousness emerge, capable of observing, feeling, questioning, and marveling at its own existence? Is there an underlying intention, a greater meaning, a cosmic purpose behind the grand unfolding of space, time, matter, and mind? This question takes us beyond the limits of empirical science, entering the domains of philosophy and spirituality, but the quantum-spiritual worldview we've constructed can offer illuminating and profoundly meaningful perspectives.

Science itself, investigating the laws and structure of the universe, has encountered an enigma suggesting, at the very least, a remarkable cosmic "conspiracy" favoring life and consciousness. This is the phenomenon of *fine-tuning*. Physicists discovered that the values of nature's fundamental constants (like the gravitational constant, the speed of light, the electron's charge, elementary particle masses) and the laws governing their interactions seem extraordinarily precise, tuned within extremely narrow margins, to allow for the existence of a complex, stable universe capable of generating stars, planets, complex chemistry, and ultimately, life as we know it. If any of these constants were slightly different, the universe would be drastically distinct and likely sterile: perhaps stars couldn't form or would burn out too quickly, perhaps carbon atoms essential for life couldn't be synthesized, perhaps the universe would have collapsed on itself or expanded too rapidly to form structures. The fact we live in a universe seemingly "tailor-made" for the existence of conscious observers like us is, to say the least, surprising.

This observation led to the formulation of the *Anthropic Principle*. In its *weak* form, it's almost a tautology: the conditions we observe in the universe must be compatible with our existence as observers, otherwise, we wouldn't be here to observe them. It's a selection bias. However, its *strong* form is more controversial and teleological (goal-oriented): it suggests the universe *must* have properties allowing life and consciousness to arise at some stage in its history. This hints that the existence of conscious observers might somehow be a "purpose" or an "embedded" outcome in the fundamental laws of the cosmos.

A popular alternative explanation for fine-tuning, avoiding the need for purpose or design, comes from the *Multiverse* hypothesis: if an infinite or vast number of parallel universes exist, each with slightly different laws and constants generated randomly, then it wouldn't be surprising that, by pure chance, some of these universes (like ours) would have the "right" conditions for life to emerge. We simply inhabit one of the "lucky" universes allowing us to exist. Yet, even the Multiverse hypothesis doesn't completely eliminate the question of purpose at a more fundamental level: why would the universe-generating mechanism produce universes with the potential for life?

Fine-tuning, however we interpret it, invites us to reflect on our place and possible significance in the grand cosmic scheme.

If modern science grapples with the enigma of fine-tuning, spiritual and philosophical traditions have, for millennia, offered direct and profound answers to the question of cosmic purpose. A recurring theme in many spiritual worldviews is that the universe exists so that primordial *Consciousness* (God, Source, Absolute, Brahman) can *experience itself* in infinite ways. Fundamental Unity, to know itself fully, manifests in multiplicity, diversity, form, limitation. Spirit ventures into matter, consciousness individualizes into myriad beings, to explore all facets of its own infinite potential through direct experience.

In Hinduism, the concept of *Lila* poetically describes the universe as the "divine play," the playful dance of Consciousness hiding and revealing itself through creation, simply for the joy of exploration and self-discovery. Other traditions emphasize purpose as the *expansion of love, creativity,* or *wisdom* in the universe. Creation would be an act of divine love, and the purpose of existence the growth in capacity to love, create, and know. Many spiritual streams also speak of a *divine plan* or a *cosmic intelligence* guiding the evolutionary process of the universe and consciousness towards a state of greater perfection, harmony, or return to the Source.

How does our individual purpose fit into this cosmic framework? If the universe exists for the experience and evolution of consciousness, then our own life, our journey as Quantum Souls, likely finds its deepest meaning when aligned with this greater purpose. We are not random accidents in an indifferent universe, but individualized expressions of universal Consciousness, with a unique role to play. Our life purpose might transcend the pursuit of material success, pleasure, or egoic recognition, and include deeper dimensions such as:

Learning and Growing: Utilizing our experiences, challenges, and relationships as opportunities to expand our wisdom, understanding, and self-awareness.

Loving and Connecting: Developing our capacity for empathy, compassion, and unconditional love, recognizing and honoring our interconnection with all beings.

Creating and Serving: Expressing our unique gifts and talents authentically, contributing to the beauty, harmony, and well-being of the world around us, serving the Whole.

Awakening: Realizing our true nature as spiritual beings, as sparks of divine Consciousness, transcending ego limitations and living from our essence.

We can use metaphors to illustrate this relationship between individual and cosmic purpose. Imagine humanity (or all conscious life) as cells in a vast cosmic organism. Each cell has its specific, specialized function, and by performing it well, contributes to the health and harmonious functioning of the whole organism. Our individual purpose would be to find and fulfill our unique function within this larger body. Or think of life as a grand cosmic play: each of us has a role to perform, with its dramas, comedies, and learnings. By playing our roles with authenticity and awareness, we not only enrich the play but also learn valuable lessons contributing to the growth of the great universal "actor" that is Consciousness itself.

Perhaps we can integrate scientific and spiritual perspectives by suggesting cosmic purpose is inherently *evolutionary* and *educational*. The universe would be a vast school of consciousness, an environment designed (or selected) to allow consciousness to arise, individualize, experience, learn, grow, and finally, awaken to its fundamental unity. The fine-tuning observed by science would be the necessary condition for this "school" to exist and function. In this scenario, by aligning ourselves with our own growth in consciousness, love, and wisdom, and by contributing to collective evolution, we are not just seeking personal fulfillment but actively participating in the greater purpose of the universe itself.

This view offers a powerful antidote to feelings of meaninglessness, alienation, or nihilism that can afflict the modern mind. The human search for purpose and meaning wouldn't be a subjective illusion, but a legitimate yearning finding validation in the very structure of a conscious, intentional cosmos. Knowing our life has cosmic purpose, that we are valuable, significant parts of a grand plan of consciousness evolution, can infuse us with a sense of dignity, resilience, and inspiration to live our lives as fully and authentically as possible. The Quantum Soul finds its deepest meaning in recognizing and embracing its role in the grandiose symphony of existence.

Chapter 32
Quantum Awakening

Throughout this exploratory journey, we've dived into the depths of the quantum universe, contemplated the mysteries of consciousness, unveiled the veils of separation between matter and spirit, and glimpsed an interconnected cosmos pulsing with purpose and evolutionary potential. We've pieced together a fascinating puzzle suggesting a reality far richer, more dynamic, and participatory than the mechanistic worldview bequeathed us.

Now, we turn our gaze to the present moment – this very instant, here in Cambé, Paraná, Brazil, on April 4th, 2025, and everywhere human consciousness breathes and seeks to understand itself. For many feel, intuitively or explicitly, that we are living through a time of profound transition, a period of potential collective awakening, where ancient truths and modern discoveries converge to catalyze a transformation in human consciousness – a true "Quantum Awakening."

This sense of change isn't just an abstract theory about scientific or philosophical paradigms; it reflects in the lived experience of countless people around the globe. Many individuals report feeling an inner "awakening," a call to a more authentic, connected way of being. This can manifest in diverse forms: growing dissatisfaction with society's purely materialistic and competitive values; a deeper search for meaning and purpose in life; heightened sensitivity to synchronicities and universal signs; a growing sense of interconnection with other humans, nature, and something larger than oneself; a desire to live with more presence, awareness, and compassion. It's as if a part of us, long dormant under layers of social conditioning and ego concerns, is beginning to awaken to our true energetic and spiritual nature.

The insights we explored in this book, emerging from the confluence of quantum physics and spiritual wisdom, act as powerful catalysts for this individual and collective awakening. Understanding we are not isolated entities, but interconnected parts of a non-local whole (as suggested by entanglement); perceiving reality not as fixed, but participatory, responding to our observation and intention; recognizing matter and spirit as integrated aspects of a single energetic reality; the possibility of consciousness transcending body and time – all these ideas have the power to shake our limiting beliefs and radically expand our perception of who we are and what is possible. This knowledge isn't merely intellectual; it reverberates through our being, inviting us to live according to this broader truth.

We can observe signs of this collective awakening manifesting in various social and cultural trends. There's a discernible movement, albeit gradual and often contested, towards re-evaluating values: a growing search for well-being over mere material wealth, for meaningful experiences over accumulation of goods, for soul-aligned authenticity and purpose over conformity to external expectations. We see a flourishing interest in self-knowledge and inner development practices like meditation, mindfulness, yoga, holistic therapies, and diverse forms of non-dogmatic spirituality, indicating a collective hunger for inner connection and transcendence. Simultaneously, social movements fighting for peace, social justice, human rights, environmental sustainability, and animal protection grow, reflecting an expanding circle of empathy and increasing awareness of our shared responsibility for the well-being of the planet and all its inhabitants.

Using quantum language metaphorically, we could say we are collectively beginning to "collapse" a new reality from the field of potentialities. For the first time in human history, a significant number of individuals have simultaneous access to both the accumulated wisdom of ancestral spiritual traditions and the revolutionary insights of modern science. This unique synthesis of intuition and reason, inner and outer knowledge, empowers us to participate in this transition more *consciously* than ever before. We are not just being carried by evolution's current; we are invited to actively row towards a more awakened future.

This feeling of being at a historical inflection point resonates with various cultural and spiritual transition narratives. New Age concepts speak of moving from the Age of Pisces to the Age of Aquarius, symbolizing a shift from paradigms based on authority and belief to paradigms of direct experience, individual freedom, and group consciousness. Indigenous prophecies from diverse cultures speak of a time of great purification and transformation on Earth, leading to a new cycle of harmony. The much-debated end of the Mayan long-count calendar cycle in 2012 was interpreted by many not as a literal world-ending event, but as a symbolic marker for the end of an old era of consciousness and the beginning of humanity's potential awakening. Regardless of these specific narratives' literal validity, they reflect a deep collective intuition that we are living in extraordinary times of change and opportunity. The focus, however, should remain on the observable transformations in consciousness and values happening here and now.

This Quantum Awakening is not a passive event happening to us; it happens *through* us. Each individual awakening to their true nature, healing their wounds, raising their vibration, and choosing to live with more awareness and love, contributes to the strength and reach of this collective movement. We are all called to actively participate by:

Cultivating self-awareness and presence through practices like meditation and mindfulness.

Embodying compassion, empathy, and forgiveness in our relationships.

Questioning and transcending limiting beliefs and obsolete paradigms, both within ourselves and society.

Consciously choosing to focus on thoughts, emotions, and intentions resonating with love, peace, unity, and understanding.

Sharing elevated knowledge and inspiring insights constructively.

Acting in the world in ways promoting healing, justice, and sustainability.

It's crucial to understand this awakening belongs to no specific religion, nation, ideology, or even a single scientific theory. It's a universal call to human consciousness to recognize its divine, interconnected essence and assume responsibility as co-creator of planetary reality. It's an invitation to transcend the divisions and fears holding us captive for so long and embrace our fundamental unity.

We undoubtedly live in challenging times, but also times of immense potential. The Quantum Awakening holds the promise that humanity can take an evolutionary leap, integrating heart wisdom with mind knowledge, science with spirit. Each of us, by awakening to our nature as a Quantum Soul, becomes a beacon of light, helping illuminate the path towards a new era of consciousness, collaboration, and harmony on our precious planet. Transformation begins within each one, but its impact is collective and potentially limitless.

Chapter 33
Quantum Soul

We reach the end of our exploratory journey, a voyage taking us from dancing subatomic particles to cosmic vastness, from consciousness mysteries to ancient wisdom traditions, from cutting-edge physics to deep spiritual experience. We've woven together threads of fundamental energy, reality's participatory nature, non-local interconnection, consciousness evolution, and the search for purpose. And at the center of this intricate tapestry emerges a luminous image of who we truly are: the Quantum Soul.

This term seeks to capture the essence of our nature as beings simultaneously integral parts of the physical universe and expressions of a vast, creative, interconnected consciousness permeating all existence. In light of all we've explored, we can now revisit and synthesize the characteristics of this Quantum Soul. It's not an ethereal, distant entity separate from the material world, but immanent and active within it, though its roots extend beyond it.

The Quantum Soul is:

Energetic and Vibrational: Its fundamental substance is the same energy composing the entire universe, vibrating at frequencies spanning matter's density to thought's and spirit's subtlety.

Conscious and Participatory: It is the seat of subjective experience, the light that perceives, feels, knows. More than that, it actively participates in creating reality through observing, intending, choosing.

Non-Local and Interconnected: Its connections transcend physical space limitations. Through principles analogous to quantum entanglement, it's intrinsically linked to other consciousnesses and the universal field of information and energy. Separation is a superficial illusion.

Potentially Timeless and Multidimensional: Its existence isn't rigidly confined to linear time flow or the three spatial dimensions we perceive. It may access, or even inhabit, a broader temporal panorama and multidimensional realities.

Informational and Holographic: It carries and processes information complexly, and perhaps, like a hologram, each individual soul contains within itself a reflection or the totality of Cosmic Consciousness.

Evolutionary and Resilient: It's on a continuous journey of learning, growth, expansion, potentially persisting beyond physical body death to continue its evolution.

It's remarkable how quantum physics itself, revealing the universe's fundamental nature, seems to provide the perfect setting for this Quantum Soul's journey. A universe not a deterministic mechanism, but a field of probabilistic potentialities, offers space for freedom of choice and learning. A universe not made of isolated objects, but an interconnected, non-local web, reflects the truth of unity and allows deep communion. A universe responding to observation and participation invites consciousness to assume its co-creator role. Modern physics, far from banishing the soul, seems to have prepared the cosmic stage for its performance.

It's crucial to understand "Quantum Soul" isn't just a poetic label for ancient spiritual concepts dressed in trendy scientific garb. It's an invitation to an *integrated identity*. It's recognizing we don't need to choose between being scientific, rational beings grounded in physical reality, *or* spiritual, intuitive beings connected to something larger. We are *both*, simultaneously. We are physical entities operating within spacetime laws, with brains and bodies needing care, *and* we are expressions of a non-local, energetic, timeless consciousness field, with access to intuition, creativity, universal connection. Living from this integrated identity means honoring all dimensions of our being, uniting reason and intuition, science and spirit, worldly action and inner connection.

From this understanding arises profound *spiritual empowerment*. The materialistic worldview often leaves us feeling like accidental cogs in a cold, meaningless cosmic machine, or powerless victims of external forces. The Quantum Soul perspective restores our dignity and agency. We are not passive spectators; we are essential participants, conscious co-creators in a living, intelligent, responsive universe. Our thoughts matter, our intentions have power, our choices shape our reality. Recognizing this frees us from helplessness and inspires us to take responsibility for our own lives and our contribution to the world.

Thus, we celebrate the great *reconciliation* between science and spirit permeating our exploration. We now see that when scientists like Einstein spoke of a "cosmic religious feeling" facing the universe's harmony and intelligibility, or expressed discomfort with quantum physics' apparent incompleteness, they were perhaps intuiting the need for a larger framework including consciousness. And when mystics of all ages described ineffable experiences of unity, inner light, connection with the Divine Source, they were perhaps directly perceiving the fundamental nature of reality science now begins glimpsing through equations and experiments. The languages differed, the methods were distinct, but the underlying truth both pointed towards might be the same: the profound unity of consciousness and cosmos.

We invite you, the reader, to allow this vision to resonate within your being. Feel yourself not just as a body *having* a soul, but as a Quantum Soul *inhabiting* and *animating* a body. You are a unique, precious expression of Universal Consciousness, a spark of cosmic fire, a being of light and information dancing through spacetime. You carry within you the heritage of stars and the infinite potential of the quantum field. Recognizing this is awakening to your true identity.

This recognition brings with it a deep *sense of purpose*, as we saw: participating in consciousness evolution, learning, loving, creating. It brings an unwavering *sense of connection*, dissolving the painful illusion of separation and revealing our unity with all life. And it brings a tender *loving responsibility*: if we are all interconnected, all part of the same Whole, then each being's well-being is inseparable from our own. We are called to act in the world with compassion, integrity, care, honoring the sacred web of existence of which we are part.

This book ends here, but your journey of self-discovery is just beginning, or perhaps, continuing with renewed vigor. May the ideas, perspectives, and practices shared here serve as a map and stimulus for your own inner and outer exploration. May you continue questioning, learning, experimenting, integrating scientific knowledge with your heart's wisdom and intuition. May you live each day with awakened awareness of your nature as a Quantum Soul, an essential, radiant part of the miracle that is the Universe. For, ultimately, the deepest truth we found is perhaps the simplest: consciousness and universe are one. And you *are* that unity.

Epilogue

Having reached this point, it's no exaggeration to say something within you has already transformed. You've traversed a journey that not only offered answers but reshaped the very questions. And that, perhaps, is the greatest gift: realizing the deepest knowledge isn't that which concludes, but that which expands. Not that which defines, but that which liberates.

You were guided across the invisible frontiers connecting matter to spirit, atom to soul, vibration to thought. And what might once have seemed fiction or ethereal spirituality now finds echo in physics equations, consciousness discoveries, the very beat of the heart.

Now you know: everything is energy. Everything vibrates. Everything is in relation. And this energy moving stars and galaxies is the same pulsing within you.

Science, with its precise tools, revealed matter is essentially space, vibration, field. Spirituality, with its silent listening, taught spirit is presence, consciousness, light. And throughout this work, these two perspectives – so often treated as opposites – were interwoven in a harmonious dance, showing what is true doesn't exclude: it complements, recognizes, unifies.

You now understand you are not a spectator of the universe, but part of it, its expression, its extension. Every thought you emit, every emotion you welcome, every intention you focus – all vibrate, resonate, transform. Reality isn't a fixed stage, but a living organism responding to consciousness's subtle touch.

And this changes everything. It changes how you relate to life. It changes how you observe events. It changes how you look at yourself.

If before the world was perceived as a succession of disconnected facts, now perhaps you see it as an energetic symphony in constant creation – where each being, each choice, each experience is a sacred note. Where you are not just the instrument, but also the musician. And, who knows, maybe even the composer.

This perception doesn't nullify suffering, nor promise a path without challenges. On the contrary: it offers depth and purpose to all that previously seemed random or chaotic. Understanding consciousness and reality dance together, you discover even pain carries a frequency, even fear possesses a vibration, and everything can be transmuted when observed with lucidity and presence.

And here lies one of this journey's greatest revelations: You are the observer. Not a passive observer, but a co-creator. Your gaze shapes. Your intention transforms. Your presence creates. This truth is liberating – but also demanding. For it returns to you what was so long projected outwards: responsibility. Responsibility for your vibration, your thoughts, your frequency. But fear not. This responsibility isn't a burden. It's a call to inner sovereignty. A reminder you are not small, limited, fragmented. You are conscious field, potential in human form, creative energy experiencing itself through time and space.

Everything you seek – peace, meaning, connection, expansion – already resides within you. Not as something to be acquired, but as something to be remembered, awakened, activated.

This book doesn't end here. Because the true journey has just begun. Now that you know reality's vibrational nature... Now that you understand the mind-matter interconnection... Now that you sense the infinity dwelling in your own being... ...the invitation is made.

Take this awareness into everyday life. Observe your thoughts like tuning a sacred instrument. Perceive your emotions as frequencies that can be modulated. Feel each instant as a unique energetic manifestation. And when the world seems dense, cold, or disconnected, remember: That is only the surface. Beneath the apparent, pulses the invisible. And the invisible is where the soul breathes, where spirit moves, where reality begins to be woven.

Continue questioning, continue feeling, continue vibrating. The "Quantum Soul" you now recognize isn't just a concept. It is you. It is everything. It is the whole in the form of presence. It is the now imbued with consciousness.

May this reading echo within you far beyond the words. May each chapter reverberate like a silent reminder of what already lives in your essence. And may, above all, you never again doubt your power to transform reality – starting from within. Because where there is consciousness, there is creation. Where there is vibration, there is possibility. And where there is you... the universe responds.

www.ingramcontent.com/pod-product-compliance
Lightning Source LLC
LaVergne TN
LVHW040052080526
838202LV00045B/3593